Albert Ball

Other books by Chaz Bowyer

Adventure in the Air, vols 1-4

Age of the Biplane

Air War Over Europe, 1939-45

Airmen of World War One

Beaufighter

Beaufighter at War

Bomber Barons

Bomber Group (No 5) at War

Bristol Blenheim

Bristol F2b

Calshot, 1913-61

Coastal Command at War

Desert Air Force at War (Co-author)

Encyclopaedia of British Military Aircraft

Eugene Esmonde VC DSO

Fighter Command, 1936-68

Fighter Pilots of the RAF, 1939-45

For Valour – The Air VCs

Gloster Meteor

Guns in the Sky – The Air Gunners

Hampden Special

Handley Page Bombers of World War One

History of the RAF

Hurricane at War

Images of Air War, 1939-45

Men of Coastal Command, 1939-45

Men of the Desert Air Force, 1940-43

Mosquito at War

Mosquito Squadrons of the RAF

Pathfinders at War

RAF Handbook, 1939-45 (and re-issue)

RAF Operations, 1918-1938

Sopwith Camel – King of Combat

Spitfire

Sunderland at War

Tales from the Bombers

The Flying Elephants

The Short Sunderland

The Wellington Bomber

Wellington at War

Edited

Adventure in the Air, vols 1-4

Bomber Pilot, 1916-1918

Enemy Coast Ahead

Fighter Pilot on the Western Front

RFC Communiques, 1917-18

The Fall of an Eagle

Wings over the Somme (and re-issue)

Albert Ball vc

Chaz Bowyer

Crécy Publishing Limited

Albert Ball VC

First published in 1977
This revised edition published in 1994 by Bridge Books, Wrexham
Reprinted in paperback in 2001 by Crécy Publishing Limited
Reprinted 2008

ISBN 9 780947 554897

Printed in England by Biddles

Crécy Publishing Limited
1a Ringway Trading Estate, Shadowmoss Road, Manchester M22 5LH
www.crecy.co.uk

CONTENTS

"...a young Esquire

Of twenty year of age, I guess...

And he had been sometime in chivalry,

In Flanders, in Artois, and in Picardy."

Chaucer

Albert Ball
VC
1896-1917

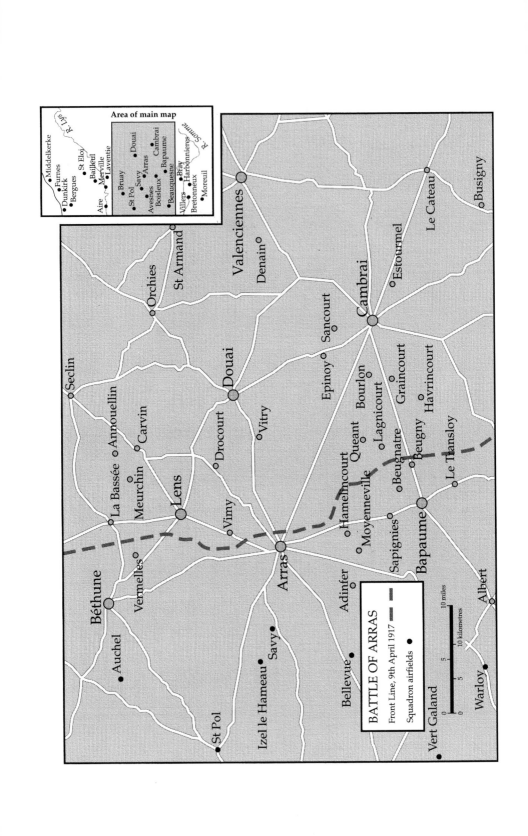

Area of main map

Middelkerke
Furnes
Dunkirk
Bergues
St Eloi
Bailleul
Merville
Aire
Laventie

Bruay
St Pol
Savy
Avesnes
Boisleux
Beauquesne
Douai
Arras
Cambrai
Bapaume
Bray
Harbonnières
Villers
Bretonneux
Moreuil

R. Lys

R. Somme

Busigny

Le Cateau

Estourmel

Valenciennes

Denain

Cambrai

St Armand

Orchies

Sancourt

Epinoy

Bourlon
Graincourt
Havrincourt
Lagnicourt
Beugny
Le Transloy

Seclin

Douai

Vitry

Queant
Beugnâtre

Annouellin
Carvin

Drocourt

Hamelincourt
Moyenneville
Sapignies

Bapaume

La Bassée
Meurchin
Lens

Vimy

Béthune

Vermelles

Adinfer

Le Transloy

Auchel

Savy

Bellevue

Albert

Izel le Hameau

Warloy

St Pol

Vert Galand

BATTLE OF ARRAS

Front Line, 9th April 1917

Squadron airfields

0   5   10 miles

0   5   10 kilometres

Acknowledgements

W ITHOUT the generous, open-handed assistance of many people, over many years, this book would hardly have been possible. The list is long but I wish to record, with deepest gratitude, my debt to each.

Primarily, I wish to express my thanks to Mrs Lois B. Anderson, sister of Albert Ball, for so graciously allowing me to invade her privacy and impose on her hospitality, and for permitting me the rare privilege of open access to the Ball family archives and private papers. Equally generous help and warm hospitality were given to me by Mrs Paddy Armstrong, Ball's niece; and Mrs Flora Thornhill, whom Albert Ball met and loved during the last few weeks of his life.

A vast amount of selfless, practical help with information, photographs, documents, contacts, and no little unpaid labour was afforded by my good friends W.B.Baguley of the Nottingham Historical Film Unit; Jack Bruce of the RAF Museum, Hendon; Norman L.R.Franks, who spent so many hours of his precious free time on my behalf poring over archival material and producing indispensable information and advice; G.Stuart Leslie 'curator' of one of the finest collections of World War One aviation photographs in existence; Mrs C.W.J.Loder of Trent College; Mrs Suella Postles of the Nottingham Castle Museum, whose enthusiasm and practical assistance were constant from the very beginning; and by no means least, Squadron Leader D.W.'Joe' Warne, RAF, chief historian of 60 Squadron RFC/RAF, whose dedication to recording history is refreshing and invaluable at all times.

Of the many individuals who contributed historical material, advice, first-hand information and accounts of Ball and his time, I would particularly thank the following listed alphabetically; R.Baker, Esq; Ralph

Barker; Wing Commander Allan Blackley, BSc, RAF, late OC 56 Squadron, RAF; Barbara Bogg; Air Commodore Keith Caldwell, CBE, MC, DFC; Flying Officer K.G. Carvosso, RAF, 11 Squadron, RAF; the late Squadron Leader Cyril M.Crowe, MC, DFC; W.O. Duncan, Esq; Flying Officer Dave Fidler, RAF; Mrs B.Fisher; Wing Commander W.Fry, MC; A.G. Harris, Esq; Squadron Leader H.E.Hervey, MC, RMS; G.Hodgkinson, Esq; Squadron Leader D.F. Holder, RAF Retired; Squadron Leader M.Jackson, OC 60 Squadron, RAF; R.H.Kiernan, Esq; Mrs E.Kitson; Mrs P.Maxfield née Hill; the late Wing Commander Gerald C.Maxwell, MC, DFC, AFC; R.C.Newman, Esq; F.P.O'Dowd, Esq; Mrs M.Poxon; W.R.Puglisi, Esq; A.Revell, Esq; B. Robertson, Esq; P.Robertson, Esq; Steve St Martin; the late Air Vice-Marshal S.F.Vincent, CB, DFC, AFC, DL; Harry Woodman.

I received enthusiastic help, combined with unfailing courtesy and efficiency, from the staffs and individuals of the following institutions and organisations; Departments AR8b and OS8b of the Ministry of Defence; Imperial War Museum; Nottingham Evening News; Public Records Office, London; Radio Nottingham; Public Archives Section of the Nottingham Reference Library; Superintendent Registrar, Nottingham; Royal Air Force Museum, Hendon; Walkers Studios, Scarborough. Finally, I would emphasise that the ultimate responsibility for all opinions, interpretations, conclusions, errors of fact or omissions within the text of this book is mine alone; and such statements should not be misconstrued as representing official opinion or any individual contributor's assessment necessarily.

Chaz Bowyer
Norwich, 1976

Introduction

To several generations, particularly his own, Albert Ball epitomised the fighter pilot. Young, audacious, apparently fearless, his fighting record shone brilliantly at a period of the devastating 1914-1918 war when British and Allied fortunes were probably at their lowest ebb. Dazed and horrified by daily reported mass carnage on the Western Front, the British population found a symbol of new hope in the deeds and fighting spirit of this youngster, who rose from obscurity to the apex of contemporary fliers in France.

Ball exemplified the offensive spirit so hardily inculcated into the Royal Flying Corps by its gruff commander Hugh Trenchard. No odds were too great for Ball to take on; no opportunity ever lost to get to grips with his country's enemies. To Albert Ball it was a simple creed - duty: to his God, his Sovereign, and especially his family. Throughout Ball's life there was no occasion when he ran from an opponent, or baulked at a challenge, unless he was literally in no position to continue. He undertook every risk encountered by his fellow fliers, and invited further dangers by always refusing to quit the field of combat until compelled to do so by circumstances beyond his control. To demur from seeking out 'the enemy' was simply unthinkable to Ball.

That his achievements and individual method of fighting inspired hundreds of his contemporaries is amply recorded in the many accounts and biographies of noted fliers published since 1918. The sheer élan and determination of Ball gave the RFC of the time an uplift in morale which was hard to surpass. More remarkably so when it is remembered that amongst his immediate contemporaries were such lion-hearted figures as Lanoe Hawker and Lionel Rees, each of whom was awarded a Victoria Cross for their prowess in aerial fighting. Yet neither of these or the many other truly great fighting pilots of the period were accorded even a worthy proportion of the publicity and adulation showered on Ball. He caught the public's imagination in a way few men ever did.

Perhaps it was the fact that Ball was essentially a lone fighter that captured the layman's phantasy; indeed, everything Ball did in his brief, crowded life marked him as the very stuff of individuality. His fighting methods owed nothing to any text book of tactics; his courage came from an inner strength, needing no artificial stimulation. Yet to label Albert Ball as a 'killer' would be to do him a gross injustice. Privately he hated his work when it involved taking a human life, as is evidenced by the many private letters he addressed to his nearest and dearest ones. Nevertheless he deliberately overcame his finer feelings in the pursuit of what he was utterly convinced was his clear duty. That call to duty led him to fight on when hindsight dictates that he was virtually exhausted in spirit and body, and should never have been permitted to return to the fighting. His quest, instigated by his own persistence, led directly to his untimely death in action.

In the sixty years since Ball's death three published biographies have been written of him (see Bibliography). Why then, the reader is entitled to ask, another biography? My answer is simple - for the sake of total accuracy and depth in subject, and therefore for posterity. My own experience in a lifetime study of aviation history has shown that - as in most facets of history - time and distance not only add a high measure of necessary objectivity in approach to any study, but can also provide much wider opportunities to unearth hitherto unpublished material. Such 'fresh' material usually establishes 'new' facts and, oft times, new facets which can alter considerably long accepted theories and 'facts'. Such has been the case with my long research on Albert Ball. The result - I trust - is a clearer picture of the man and, certainly, his life and Service record.

History is a haven for distorted memories and legend - witness the many respected academics who so firmly believed the first man to 'discover' the Piltdown Skull - but in this book I set out to establish facts. Thus the reader will undoubtedly find herein certain statements and data which differ from long-held beliefs about Ball and his career. All have been scrupulously checked with original and unquestionable authentic sources. Whilst not primarily concerned with scotching legends, inevitably a conscientious biographer must seek out the truth, and this has been my only criterion. Nevertheless, I am only too conscious that revealing unvarnished truth can so easily destroy long cherished beliefs held by those intimately concerned with the subject, and it is not my prime intention to cruelly shatter private chimera.

From its earliest years my generation grew up familiar with the names, deeds, and example, of such men as Edward 'Mick' Mannock, VC, 'Jimmy' McCudden, VC, Oswald Boelcke, Werner Voss, 'Eddie' Rickenbacker, Georges Guynemer and, in my case particularly, a boy called Albert Ball. These were just some of a myriad of inspiring names in an era which saw the emergence of aviation as man's latest, greatest achievement. If this book helps in some way to perpetuate them in a modern schoolboy's imagination, I shall be content. If too it helps to emphasise to coming generations of young men the madness and awesome waste of human resources inherent in war; the pointless sacrifice of too many generations' fine young men and women on the altar of political greed and old men's shallow pride, then I shall be doubly content.

Chaz Bowyer
Norwich, 1976

Preface to the 1994 Edition

W HEN the first edition of this volume was written my prime intention was to place on record the military service of Albert Ball as accurately as possible, rather than offer a 'full' biography. In my view the latter, as applied to a boy who died before attaining his majority, could mean very little in comparison with his achievements as a pilot. Thus, in this latest edition, I have merely 'tidied up' minor literal errors, but have taken the opportunity to greatly expand the pictorial content.

Inevitably, with the passing of time since that first edition, certain individuals who co-operated in my researches have now passed on. Of these, Mrs Lois Anderson, Ball's sister, died on 7th March 1984, while Keith 'Grid' Caldwell died on 28th November 1980, 'Tim' Hervey on 30th May 1990 and 'Willie' Fry on 4th August 1992.

Chaz Bowyer
Norwich, 1994

1

Schooldays

VIZEFELDWEBEL Jäger glanced towards his three companions. Each, like himself, was virtually unrecognisable in bulky fur-lined coats and swathing scarves; their heads mis-shapen in outline by creased leather flying helmets and glinting eye goggles. The four sleek Albatros scouts of *Jagdstaffel* 20 gently undulated up and down as they began gradually to lose height from 10,000 feet, flying south eastwards towards the shell-ruined French town of Cambrai. The evening dusk was just beginning to infiltrate the fading daylight, with a soft ground mist slowly diffusing the earth pattern below. Jäger was tired. It had been an uneventful patrol, with no incident worthy of note, and now, well over German occupied territory with some twenty-five miles to go to the *Staffel*'s base airfield at Guise, he was unconsciously relaxing from the past ninety minutes of constant, neck-stretching vigilance. In perhaps fifteen minutes' time he would be climbing stiffly out of his cold open cockpit, with the pleasing prospect of an evening in the Mess room ahead amongst good comrades.

At that moment, one thousand feet higher, unnoticed by the quartet of red-painted German scouts, a lone Nieuport pilot pivoted his tiny biplane on its left wing tips, and plunged straight down at the centre of the enemy formation. As the nearest Albatros loomed large in his Aldis gunsight the bare-headed pilot fired a brief burst from his wing-mounted Lewis machine gun. Its effect was immediate as all four German pilots reacted instinctively, heeling away from this totally unexpected onslaught, each banking frantically out of the danger zone. Within seconds the silver Nieuport slid underneath Jäger's

Albatros and, with his Lewis gun now slanted upwards on its mounting, its pilot slammed two and a half drums of ball and tracer bullets into the ply-covered fuselage just above him at almost point-blank range. The red Albatros veered erratically, seemingly paused, then tumbled down from the sky to crash near a small crossroads junction just south of Sancourt village, three miles north of Cambrai.

As the Nieuport climbed away, Jäger's companions, recovered from their initial shock, attempted to avenge their lost friend and bore in from different angles to attack the solitary enemy. With comparative ease the Nieuport pilot at first out-manoeuvred and then out-climbed his opponents, before setting course for his own airfield. Bereft of ammunition, he had little choice but to return to base. His name was Albert Ball, and the date May 6th 1917. Almost exactly twenty-four hours later Ball crashed to his death behind the German lines and thus abruptly, tragically, terminated a brilliant fighting career which had made him a household name. Only twenty years old when he died, in the final fifteen months of his life Albert Ball had risen from obscure reconnaissance pilot to the foremost rank of contemporary Allied fighter pilots; his name had become synonymous with courage.

Albert Ball's origins gave little hint of his future fame. His father, Albert, born on July 20th 1863, was the son of George Ball, a native of Lenton, near Nottingham, whose profession was plumbing engineer. Following in his father's footsteps, Albert too became a master plumber, and on July 19th 1886 married Harriet Mary Page, a Derby girl who was the daughter of Henry Page, a mechanic. The first child of the marriage, a daughter whom they named Hilda, was born on August 16th 1887, but tragically died only days after her first birthday in the following year. Four years later, on February 26th 1892, a second daughter, Lois Beatrice, was born. The first son of the marriage, christened Albert after his father, and the subject of this book, was born on August 14th 1896, in

His fate unknowing...Albert Ball as a baby, 1896

the Ball home at 301 Lenton Boulevard (now retitled Castle Boulevard). A fourth child, Arthur Cyril, was born on January 10th 1898.

Albert Ball senior was an ambitious man and, by the turn of the century, changed his profession to become an estate agent and general dealer in land and properties; establishing his first office at 9 Cheapside, Nottingham. By that time he had also entered local politics and, from November 1899, was a city councillor for the Castle Ward of Nottingham. By 1905 he was appointed a Justice of the Peace, and four years later he was elected Mayor of Nottingham, the first of four terms in that office during his lifetime.* In June 1912 he became an alderman on the Nottingham city council, and indeed served on a wide variety of city and council committees throughout his life.

---

* 1909; 1910; 1920 (part) 1935-36. The office was retitled as Lord Mayor from 1927.

Ball as a pupil at Lenton Church School, 1904

His long public service record was eventually recognised by a knighthood in the 1924 New Year's Honours List.

Harriet Ball, a devoted mother and wife, had come from respectable forebears of modest but relatively comfortable means, and as her husband prospered and steadily rose in the local social scale, she adapted naturally to her increasingly responsible role as the wife of a dignitary and successful business man. Nor were her duties confined to her immediate family, but included filling the civic office of Mayoress to her bachelor brother-in-law for a period.

The family soon moved from Lenton Boulevard to take up residence in Sedgley House, a high-gabled building with reasonably extensive gardens in the select Park district of Nottingham. A few minutes easy stroll from the east walls of the imposing Nottingham Castle, Sedgley looked out due south high over the adjacent Nottingham Canal, with the winding River Trent in the near distance. In Sedgley House the three Ball children grew up in genteel surroundings with all the appurtenances associated with moderate wealth. Young Albert occupied a room at the top rear of the house which remained his own, even after his death, as long as the family occupied the house. All three children benefited from the love and indulgence of a close-knit family life. Their father, hard-headed and subjective in all matters of pure commerce, was extraordinarily patient, even lenient, with them; though in the tenor of the period, remained the master in his own house. Fiercely protective of his offspring, he unfailingly supported them in all things, and willingly assumed responsibility for any nuisance or annoyance caused by his lively children. From their mother, the youngsters received the fullest measure of maternal love, and reciprocated that devotion.

They were undoubtedly happy days for young Albert, who quickly developed into a robustly healthy boy, with an apparently unquenchable taste for fresh adventures, and possessing an intense curiosity about things in the mechanical and engineering fields. Behind the house was a small wooden shed in which Albert was given free rein to indulge his curiosity and conduct his many experiments. The boy filled the hut with radio and morse equipment, electrical gadgetry, and a small bench on which he and his young friends would often dissect near-defunct petrol engines and patiently rebuild these until they coaxed a spark of life back into the machinery.

Albert soon joined the growing Boy Scout movement, becoming a patrol leader in the local troop which had its headquarters in an empty shop in Willoughby Street, Lenton, under the supervision of a friend, Robert Norris. On several occasions Albert brought his patrol to Sedgley House, there to enlist their labour in his various experiments, and 'rewarding' them with a sticky cream tea, served sedately by a housemaid.

Yet another early fascination was kite flying, his first connection with the art of flight in any form, and he eventually accomplished 'one-kite power' by trailing a large kite across nearby parkland and using the pull of the guide string to propel him along on his bicycle – an exhilarating experience.

Encouraged by a doting father, Albert was instructed in the use of firearms and permitted to practise with hand guns, firing at targets or sticks set up in the gardens of Sedgley House. A natural shot, and possessing exceptionally keen eyesight, Albert quickly developed into a precise marksman, early evidence of his later prowess with guns in aerial combat.

The boy's taste for novel experiences unconsciously displayed a major characteristic – a perfectly natural lack of fear in what ordinarily might be considered dangerous situations. On his sixteenth birthday, for example, he accepted eagerly an invitation from a local steeplejack, George Timms, to accompany him in climbing to the top of a very tall industrial chimney stack. Once at the top, Albert coolly walked around the rim as if merely strolling down a street, enthralled with the novelty of his 'bird's-eye view' of his home town, and excitedly pointing out familiar landmarks.

The boy's academic schooling comprised a series of disruptive changes and varying emotions. Certainly in his younger years Albert was never entirely happy away from his family. His love for them never left him throughout his brief life, whilst his deep devotion to his mother was unceasing. With his younger brother Cyril, he first became a pupil of the Lenton Church School. From there he progressed to Grantham Grammar School, but soon moved on to Nottingham High School.

Finally, in January 1911, both Albert and Cyril were enrolled in Trent College at Long Eaton, near

Nottingham. Albert was initially allotted to F Dormitory (retitled Hanbury House in 1914) and became a member of Form Vc under the tutorship of G J Thomas; whilst Cyril joined the same dormitory though in a junior form.

Trent College had originally opened in April 1868 as an institution for the education of the sons of Church of England parents. Its raison d'etre was to teach the faith's 'original principles... without hindrance and without intolerance' – a direct challenge to the contemporary Oxford Movement as embodied in Doctor Woodard and the new schools which his influence had created.

When the Ball brothers entered the college its headmaster was John Savile Tucker, an austere, remote man with strict ideas on discipline and moral welfare; ideas to which he required strict adherence by both staff and pupils. With annual fees of only £75 it was not altogether surprising that Tucker's long regime was one of austerity, but to boys like Albert and Cyril Ball, raised in comfortable surroundings and indulged by generous parents, the daily disciplined routine of the college came

Trent College

Trent College scholars. Ball is 3rd from left, back row

Cyril (left) and Albert Ball at Trent College

as something of a jolt. Throughout the year, irrespective of weather or temperature, the first bell for awakening was sounded at 6.25am, to be followed immediately by compulsory cold baths for all. The daily fare was frugal, and almost invariably supplemented by privately purchased 'tuck'. Domestic central heating was seldom effective in the winter months, creating near-arctic temperatures in dormitory and classroom. Internal lighting was all by gas, no electricity was used in the college then.

Physical exercise was a constant creed, exemplified in part by the regular (and again compulsory) long walks for all pupils and staff; cross-country runs for the whole college; and even to the lower levels of approved punishment for boys committing any misdemeanour in the shape of 'penal drills', periods of sheer physical exercises in the gymnasium. Higher up the scale of possible punishments came a beating with a fives bat from either a

Ball with his home-made punt on the Nottingham Canal

Albert Ball outside the Trent College Armoury, 1911

prefect or a master; whilst the ultimate punishment, reserved by Tucker for his exclusive application, was a 'swishing', administered in the Head's classroom, with or without benefit of trousers, by a long cane kept solely for this purpose. Trivial offences were dealt with by the time-honoured dreary labour of writing 'lines'.

Academically Trent taught most of the basic subjects expected of a minor public school, but perhaps its true value lay in its 'teaching' the abstract values of life. By example and inference, Trent taught Albert Ball ideals in many facets of life, not least being the ideal of duty. The college's basic theme could be summed up in the phrase, 'Manners makyth Man', and this 'motto' undoubtedly appealed greatly to Albert's maturing outlook.

Never a star pupil in book matters, Ball preferred to

Ball, aged 15, relaxing in the garden of the family home, Sedgley House, Nottingham

utilise his abundant energy in a wide variety of non-academic activities. In Albert's years at Trent (1911-13) the college's chief sport was association football (soccer).* Though Albert himself took little real interest in sporting activities as such, he dutifully entered for many athletic events in the various inter-dormitory competitions, even winning a small silver cup for his success in an obstacle race.

Instead he took up photography, carpentry, music lessons on the violin, modelling in wood and metal, indeed, any subject which offered the chance to use hands and brain in co-ordination. Idleness, either in mind or body, was never a trait in Ball. Selected extracts from some of the many letters he wrote to his family during his

* In late 1914, this was changed to Rugby Football.

time at Trent – always couched in spelling which, despite the endeavours of his masters, remained firmly his own – reveal some of the diverse subjects with which he occupied a full school life.

> Well, this afternoon I have been navvying. It was very nice. I have made a very good switchboard, and also have invented an accumulator for pocket lamp... I have just finished my prep and have written an essay. Oh you can imagine how pleased I was to get my camera. I took a grand photo yesterday. I gave myself proper time and try not to do too many at once. I had occasion to mend my camera with the help of my

Ball's first taste of military discipline, as cadet in the Trent College Officers Training Corps (OTC), 1913.

master yesterday. The damp has made the bellows leak a little but I made a good job of it... Well, I am really getting on fine with your medicine chest. I cut the back out today and shall soon fasten it to the frame, but it is no good hurrying in carpentry. I mean to try and bring home a serviceable and good article with me... This term I have been making a model electric launch. It carries 48lb and is looking very decent. I have also devoted two hours a week to machine-drawing. I am now able to draw quite decently, and also understand a drawing.

Life at Trent was not all smooth sailing for Ball. His immature ideals of fair play and common justice were often rudely cracked by day to day incidents, as witnessed in a note he wrote home in the early days.

I am getting on very nicely at school just now, but there has been a little bother on in the carpenter's shop. There has been a boy who broke a strap and he would not own up to it. So about six boys about eighteen years old came and held us all down and spanked us.

Well, we are going to hide now so that they cannot catch us. I shall be pleased when 26 more days have passed away...

This last ironic comment referred to an imminent holiday when Ball would rejoin his family at Sedgley House; a college rule at that time forbade parents from visiting Trent except on traditional Speech Days. It might have been the result of some similar 'injustice', real or imagined, or simply an innate quest for new adventure, but on at least one occasion Albert deserted the college, and was eventually traced to the port of Liverpool where he was discovered, '... covered in coal dust, in the engine room of an outgoing steamer.'

In the main, however, Ball was reasonably content with his schooling, but by 1912 was beginning to think in terms of his future career. In a letter to his mother that year he wrote, in part:

> I have a great love for my school and shall be sorry in many ways to leave, but I think that if I get into a good business I shall be spending my life in a much more profitable way and bringing out the best in myself... I am anxious to know what I shall be when I leave, and I do hope father is looking about well. I think there is a lot of money to be made in the way of making small electric-lighting plants for country houses... I should like to be placed in a large electrical engineering factory where they make all kinds of machinery...

In view of Albert's stirring ambition, his parents persuaded him to broach the matter with his headmaster. Shortly after, Ball wrote:

> I had an interview with the Head and he said that I am to do extra maths, also drawing. He advised me to start on the practical end of engineering, then after I have had a year at that I can take to theory, then try to pass an exam. Well, the Head thinks that engineering is the right thing, so if it pleases you, I will be an electrical engineer.

Buckling down to his extra year at Trent, Albert studied hard. He also joined the college Officers Training Corps (OTC), his first experience of 'Army' life and its regulated routine. He was not too impressed, but considered it an obligation, hence a form of duty to his school, and his family.

Ball finally left Trent College at the end of the 1913 summer term. He was then just seventeen years of age. Physically he had matured into a strong, stockily-built young man, and reached his full height of five feet six inches. His urge to start spending his life 'in a much more profitable way' was not entirely focussed on any specific or prime desire to accumulate wealth. He had, from his father's example, a healthy respect for money as a means to several ends, but regarded it mainly as a necessary basic 'tool' in any commercial career. From his father too he had inherited an intuitive business instinct which was variously manifested in the coming years.

With the help and influence of his parents, Ball began in business with the Universal Engineering Works, a small electrical and brass-founding concern situated in Castle Boulevard, Nottingham. Here he was happy, busying himself learning, experimenting, and feeling, with all the abundant self-confidence of any healthy seventeen-year old, that he was now a fully-fledged member of his father's world of commerce. The months slipped by with Ball excited in his new, larger existence, his imagination filled with plans for his future. His plans – like those of so many millions of other young men – were never to reach fruition. A thousand miles from Nottingham there were rumblings of revolution and political intrigue, harbingers of the most disastrous war in the history of the human race.

By early 1914 the political atmosphere on the European continent was deteriorating rapidly. Diplomatic intrigue amongst the various empires and entities was inexorably eroding decades of peaceful co-existence, and an era was poised on the brink of self-destruction.

On June 28th Archduke Francis Ferdinand of Austria was assassinated in Sarajevo, and this murder provoked an Austrian ultimatum to Serbia, whose government was alleged (by Austria) to have organised the 'subversive movement' responsible for the killing of Austria's heir-apparent. With the tacit support of Kaiser Wilhelm of Germany, Austria finally declared war on Serbia on July 28th 1914. This act inevitably sparked off a chain reaction involving Russia, Germany and France, whose various intertwined treaties of mutual support in the event of war soon involved Britain too.

Despite many attempts by Britain to calm the explosive situation, Kaiser Wilhelm of Germany merely exacerbated the threat of catastrophe by declaring war on Russia on August 1st, and within hours issued an ultimatum to Belgium to permit passage of the German army through Belgian territory with the object of attacking Russia's ally, France.

Britain guaranteed armed support to Belgium in the event of any German violation of Belgian neutrality, and on August 3rd the British government ordered a general

The Ball children. Albert (left), Lois Beatrice and Cyril

*Posing in the garden of Sedgley House with "trophies",
including a silver cup won in a college obstacle race*

mobilisation of her armed services and reserve formations. On the following day, at 11pm (BST), Britain was officially at war with Germany.

Britain's reasons for becoming embroiled in the Continental cataclysm were given on August 6th by the Prime Minister in the House of Commons. 'In the first place to fulfil a solemn international obligation... secondly, to vindicate the principle... that small nationalities are not to be crushed by the arbitrary will of a strong and over-mastering Power.'

It was a blatant appeal to the upholding of national honour, and the British population responded in huge volume. Alone amongst the European great powers in not having conscription as an integral facet of her Services' recruitment – a legacy from the Duke of Wellington a century before, who had laid down the dictum that British Army recruits for 'foreign service' must be volunteers – the British government launched an immediate nationwide appeal for volunteers to fight against Germany.

On August 7th there first appeared the most famous recruiting poster in British Service history – Field Marshal Lord Kitchener's stern face, ample moustache and extended forefinger, over the blunt message, *'Your Country Needs YOU'*. Kitchener followed this with a more specific appeal – for an 'addition to His Majesty's Regular Army' of 100,000 men, aged between 19 and 30, for 'general service for a period of three years, or until the War is concluded.' The response was prodigious, and by September 15th 1914, Kitchener's 'New Army' had already enlisted half a million young men; each an eager volunteer.

In Nottingham during the early days of that fateful August local dignitaries and prominent citizens drew huge crowds to meetings solely intended as recruitment rallies. Albert Ball, just about to celebrate his eighteenth birthday, was but one of many hundreds of local lads who eagerly volunteered to fight for King and Country. Within a few weeks he was called to the colours and on September 21st 1914, enlisted in the 1st Platoon, A Company, of the 2/7th Battalion, Nottinghamshire and Derby Regiment* as a private soldier, in the ranks.

---

* Known more familiarly as 'The Sherwood Foresters', and formerly titled 'The Robin Hood Rifles'.

2

Fledgling Wings

THE first few weeks of the war were filled with confusion and bustle as a leisurely peacetime Army administration attempted manfully to cope with the sudden influx of more men than already existed in the service. Accommodation, kitting, organisation, preparation, training; a myriad of details inherent with the manipulation of many thousands of raw recruits, all took time and unprecedented effort. Albert Ball's battalion was billeted locally in Nottingham, and commenced elementary drill training in nearby Wollaton Park and the drill hall in Derby Road.

Within days of first donning khaki serge uniform, Ball was promoted to sergeant, in view of his boy scout knowledge of field lore, and particularly his experience and training in Trent College OTC. His age and youthful appearance contrasted quaintly with such senior rank, with its normal corollary of long experience and mature responsibility, but the majority of his 'men' were hardly older. To Ball it seemed no more than the authority of a prefect in charge of other senior boys. Nevertheless, he took his duties seriously and privately revelled in leading his soldiers in local field exercises and training syllabuses. On October 28th he relinquished his three chevrons on being appointed to a commission as Second Lieutenant, with effect from the following day.

The days and nights of the first winter of the war passed quickly for Ball – drill, field exercises, mock skirmishes with nearby troops, route marches – indeed, the normal basic training for 'rookies' in the service. To Ball, like every man in uniform at that time, it was an impatient, frustrating time; waiting for the call to active service in France, and a 'fear' that the war would be over before he had a chance to see fighting action.

On January 1st 1915, with a hope of accelerating his eventual move to the fighting zone, Ball was seconded to the North Midlands Divisional Cyclist Company (NMDCC). Thoroughly at home at the wheel of an automobile or motor cycle, a skill shared with his sister, Lois, who was only the second woman in Nottingham to qualify for a driver's licence, Ball was first posted to Bishop's Stortford, Hertfordshire, during February 1915, being billeted in South Road there for some weeks. His urgent wish to join the 'real war' in France continued to be frustrated, however, and he had to be content with training his men, playing in mock wars locally, and watching droves of other soldiers being despatched to the fighting.

In a letter home dated February 24th, he complained:

> I am very disappointed just now. I have just sent five boys to France, and I hear that they will be in the firing line by Monday. It is just my luck to be unable to go. Well, Captain Black says that I shall go with the first draft of reserves, which goes from here in a month's time. I may go before if we lose more of the men who are at the front. It is surprising what a lot of the brave fellows are killed every day. I notice that it is mostly the best men who are killed in every case... Ten thousand are leaving for France tonight.

On March 8th, writing again from Bishop's Stortford, Ball struck a happier note:

> I have just received orders to get ready for the Reserve. I have to pack up at once and get off to Luton. This is going to be a nice big job, but it is ripping to be doing a bit of something we know is real.

At Luton, Ball continued a daily routine of training, preparing other men for the fighting line, and on April 28th wrote to his sister Lois – 'Dearest Lol' to Albert on a slightly more serious note, 'I do hope they will soon let us loose in France. I do not think they will be very long. Nearly all the cyclists who went from Bishop's Stortford are either killed or wounded.' He then added a completely unconscious touch of ironic humour, 'It will be fine when we go...' In the meantime he busied himself with a variety of routine duties, including taking charge of the service canteen finances and converting a deficit into a profit account – an example of his natural business instinct being put to practical use.

In June 1915 Ball was sent on a platoon officers' training course to Perivale, Middlesex, just north-west of London. Accommodation was tented, in an open field, but by now Ball was thoroughly versed in Army discomforts. It was while he attended this instructional course that his thoughts first turned seriously to the possibilities of flying. Apart from any personal desire to taste a new experience, flying offered another possible means of getting to the fighting in France. Increasing casualties and the rapidly expanding establishment within the Royal Flying Corps offered, at least, an opportunity.

About four miles north of Perivale was Hendon aerodrome, the mecca of would-be fliers hoping to join the Royal Flying Corps or Royal Naval Air Service eventually. At Hendon were several civilian flying schools which, for a private fee of £75 to £100, trained men to the necessary pilot standards required to qualify for a Royal Aero Club Pilot Certificate – a necessary pre-requisite at that time before acceptance for further Service flying instruction in either of the two air services.

For Ball, enrolment for flying instruction was a private matter which could not be permitted to interfere with his normal service duties. Thus, having enrolled in the Ruffy-Baumann School at Hendon, Ball began a schedule of wakening at 3am, motor-cycling on a noisy Harley-Davidson to Hendon as dawn broke, and snatching anything from a few minutes to an hour of elementary pilot instruction, wind and weather permitting, before returning to Perivale in time for the first parade of the day there at 6.45am.

This decision was entirely his own, and he had already paid a deposit on his ultimate fee, and commenced instruction under the skilful guidance of Edouard Baumann, before mentioning the new venture to his family. In a letter dated July 4th 1915, he announced casually:

> I go in for a little flying now and find it great sport. I had a fall yesterday but I soon got straight again and went up in another machine. Please do not be very cross with me for flying, for it means that if the country is very short of pilots I shall be able to go.

In a separate letter to his father, he explained:

> Well, you asked me to let you know all about my flying. I am only too pleased to let you know, for I am getting on fine. I go to Hendon every morning at 4 o'clock, and I hope to pass for my ticket in a few weeks. If I pass I get £60 back from the RFC. In the first place you have to pay £75. I have paid £10. I love flying, and as they are very short of pilots, I may do a little good… I think I shall make a good pilot.

In the event his expressed hope to take his 'ticket' (Royal Aero Club Certificate tests) 'in a few weeks' was slightly optimistic, and it was to be nearly four months before that occasion. At the Ruffy-Baumann School he was first given elementary instruction in aircraft controls and handling, including a few short flights around the perimeter of the airfield, by Clarence Winchester, and then continued

M.Edouard Baumann who, among others, taught Ball to fly at Hendon

his pure flying instruction under Edouard Baumann. The aircraft used were single-engined tractor machines, loosely based on the small Caudron design, with a single engine of either 50 or 60 horse-power. Pupil and instructor sat in the tiny nacelle behind the engine, in tandem cockpits.

As an embryo pilot, Ball showed no particular aptitude, and was no worse – or better – than the average student, but his enthusiasm for this new mode of locomotion was great.

Like all student pilots of the period, he was often to suffer agonies of frustration when, having arrived at dawn, eager for his next brief lesson, he was told 'No flying, the wind's too strong'. The frail, ultra-light training machines were too low-powered to entrust to any condition of winds exceeding 5-8mph in strength, and produced their best performance in non-windy circumstances. Thus, the pupils often only accumulated a few minutes actual

airborne instruction over relatively long periods of days –
just one factor in the length of time it finally took Ball
(and his fellow pupils) to reach the 'ticket' stage.

The dawn excursions, exposed to wind and weather, on
the saddle of an oily motorcycle, along roads which threw
up clouds of dust and dirt, did little to enhance Ball's
appearance in terms of Service smartness.

Blissfully unconscious of this, Ball was somewhat taken
aback to be reprimanded by his immediate senior, as he
explained to his family with typical honesty – in a letter:

> Our CO sent for me this morning and said,
> 'Ball, you have got many things to learn'. He told
> me that I had got to come dressed in a clean
> uniform and not in any oily things. Well, he is
> giving me until Monday, so I shall have to give up
> looking like work and go like a nut. It seems
> strange, but it is so, and I shall have to see that rules
> are carried out. All the other chaps are dressed
> well, so I shall have to put a clean uniform on.

By the beginning of August Ball had completed his
army course at Perivale and returned to his own platoon,
based at Shafford's Farm, St Albans, some twenty miles
north of Hendon. The added distance did not interfere
with his routine of rising before dawn to motor-cycle to
the airfield, and then return to camp to commence a full
day of normal duties. With the long summer evenings Ball
often returned to Hendon at the end of the day for further
instruction. The inherent dangers of flying were soon
brought home to Ball when he witnessed several crashes
in which pupils were often seriously injured or, on
occasion, killed. Another of his near-daily letters home
described one such occasion.

> Well, my flying is going on fine, but I am very
> sorry to say that a great many of our men have been
> killed in the last few weeks. It is rotten to see the

Caudron G2 trainer as used by the Ruffy-Baumann School, Hendon

smashes. Yesterday, a ripping boy had a smash, and when we got up to him he was nearly dead, he had got a two-inch piece of wood right through his head and died this morning. If you would like a flight I should be pleased to take you anytime you wish.

The final comment, made in all innocence of its irony, demonstrated how little Ball feared for his own safety, and exemplified his self-confidence.

In a further note to his sister, he wrote:

I was so pleased to get your ripping cake, but I have nearly finished it. I love to take a huge piece with me when I fly. I cannot say when I shall take my ticket. I saw a rotten smash yesterday, a boy came down 200 feet, smashed his arm in three places, and nearly got burned to death. I am going on fine.

Ball, throughout his life, was a prodigious letter writer, though none were ever very long. It was not because he particularly enjoyed writing, indeed, many of his letters were no more than a single page or even less filled with his large sloping scripthand, but he felt an obligation, even a duty, to keep in constant touch with his beloved family. In writing to his mother he seldom included anything which might cause her concern or worry, such was his deep love for her. To his father he tended to be slightly more formal; a natural respect for his paternal elder. But to his sister, Lois – 'Dearest Lol' – he often opened his heart, and usually described items and events which would possibly have distressed or caused unnecessary parental concern had he included such matters in their letters. Lois was his confidante, and Albert felt much closer to her in spirit than to his younger brother, Cyril; though this may partly have been the natural feeling of an older brother to a younger brother. In a letter to his father dated August 10th he said,

You do make me laugh by sending such very serious letters. If I took life as serious as you do, I should be dead by tomorrow. However, as you say, when I do think, I quite see that you only preach in order to do me good.

Yet in a letter to his mother soon after, his mood was confined, as always, to lighter things:

When am I going to get a letter from you, they do seem a long time in coming. Do please let me have a long one, with heaps of news, and a big cake. You make me a cake, and I would like it all the more. I so love to have a huge piece of cake to go flying with in the morning. It is fine, and if made by you would be better still. I am having a ripping time. All our School machines are in order now.* I am having a morning off to write letters, for I do not often like writing, and when I do it is best for me to get to work at once.

Ball's objective, his RAeC 'ticket', continued to be delayed due to the capricious weather, but in part due to increasingly heavier duties with his platoon. During August and September he was only able to average two flying lessons each week, but remained determined to gain his certificate. Finally, on October 15th came the longed-for tests. Flying a school Caudron, Ball passed the various test manoeuvres with ease, and in due course was awarded Royal Aero Club Certificate No. 1898.** In a letter to his father on that date he wrote:

* In a letter to his father dated September 15th, he had remarked, '... all our machines have been smashed up three times.'

** This certificate, the details of which were completed by an anonymous clerk at the Royal Aero Club, made the curious mistake of recording Ball's birthdate as August 21st 1896. When Ball eventually received his certificate and signed it, he did not correct the date. Even more curious, however, was the repetition of this incorrect date by the official historian, H A Jones, and subsequent biographers, who simply perpetuated this error. Ball's birth certificate – Entry No 162 in the Register of Birth No 37, Nottingham (South West) Sub-District – confirms the correct birthdate.

Ball posing at Hendon on being awarded his initial pilot's RAeC Certificate

It is now Thursday morning, and through the wind blowing so much on Monday and Tuesday I have not got my ticket yet. I did some ripping flying by myself this morning, but now the wind is up again, but I shall stay on the ground all this afternoon, and if it drops for half-an-hour I am going up for my ticket. Lois and Cyril came down, but only saw me do straights. We went up to town (London) yesterday and I called at the War Office and was told that I was in the Flying Corps and should be told when to report in a few days. I have had to send a cheque for £1 10s in order to be in the Royal Flying Corps. Please excuse short note as I am very excited.

Despite Ball's statement that he was now in the RFC, in fact he was on secondment only for a probationary period, his ultimate transfer depending entirely on how he fared during his Service flying training, and on his successfully qualifying for a pilot's brevet ('wings') at the finish.

On October 23rd he reported to No 9 Reserve Squadron, a training unit, at Mousehold Heath aerodrome, just north of Norwich, Norfolk, and on the same day had his first flying experience in a Service machine. His reaction was not unexpected, '… It is fine piloting these huge machines, after flying the old crocks at Hendon.' To his surprise he was billeted in relative luxury in the Royal Hotel, Norwich initially, but was soon after moved to a more mundane private house in Riverside Road, fronting a section of the River Wensum. Not caring too much for either his billet, the food served, or the company there, he again changed billets for another private house in Thorpe Road, Norwich.

For his first two weeks at Mousehold Heath he did virtually no flying, due to heavy rains and squalls predominating the weather conditions. At the beginning of November he, and the other embryo RFC pilots, were offered a chance to go to France within four weeks, provided they ceased pilot training and became flying observers – the equivalent of air gunners. No 18 Squadron RFC, equipped with Vickers FB5 two-seat 'pusher' aircraft, was about to join the war in France that month, and needed trained observers to make up its full complement of air crews.

Ball seriously considered this offer, but in the end declined. Apart from his determination to complete his training as a pilot, his business instinct rejected any waste of money and time already spent. As he put the matter in a letter home:

> It really is a great temptation, but I think as I had paid for my course at Hendon, etc, I had better wait and go as a pilot.

When the weather permitted, Ball and his fellow pupils continued their instruction, both in the air and the lecture huts. Ball, for all his keenness and enthusiasm, learned slowly, and had his share of mishaps – a constant corollary to flying training in 1915, when the 'art' of instruction at RFC training units was still rather haphazard and certainly unco-ordinated when compared with the 1917-18 period. He once crashed from 800 feet (due to loose control wires) but looked on the whole incident as something to be laughed at, and sent home a splintered strut from the wreckage, the first of many 'souvenirs' to be despatched to Nottingham during the coming year. In terms of accomplishing the natural lightness of control and instinctive co-ordination of hands, feet and brain when in complete mastery of an aeroplane, Ball was a 'late developer'.

During the first week of December, after an all-night duty as orderly officer, he reported to the airfield and was told by an instructor to take up an aircraft solo. Climbing into a Maurice Farman, No 418, Ball took off joyfully, climbed to 300 feet and then attempted a landing. The landing was anything but good, and the instructor promptly vented his spleen on the hapless Ball, suggesting that he seek a good girls' flying school for further elementary instruction!

At this burst of totally undeserved sarcasm Ball lost his temper. Pointing out, in forcible terms, that he had only fifteen minutes' experience in this type of aircraft, he ended his blistering riposte by saying that if he could not be given decent instruction then he would far rather return to the Cyclists Company. The instructor relented, had another machine wheeled out, and Ball proceeded to complete five good landings in a row, thus satisfying his honour, and convincing the testy instructor of his potential.

Describing one crash in which he was involved, Ball unwittingly revealed his characteristic lack of fear in 'tight' situations:

> I feel rotten today, but just feel like writing. Well, you know by now about my smash; it was a good one. They say I crashed to earth at 120 miles an hour, and to look at the undercarriage I should think that I did; however, it is nearly ready for flying again now. It was a rum feeling coming down, for I had time to see that my number was up; however it is not!

Neither this crash, or any of his previous mishaps, ruffled Ball's outlook on becoming a pilot; he simply accepted them as his personal 'ration' of incidents which occurred to the majority of pupils. By the end of November he was beginning to show great improvement in his handling, and understanding, of an aeroplane, and was exploring a variety of manoeuvres and capabilities of his machines. A letter dated December 5th gives an inkling of his increasing skill and self-confidence:

> I have been allowed to do a great deal of work. I started my day of success by flying for half an hour in the clouds. Well, as you know, when in the clouds you cannot see land, or even sky. However I stuck to my machine and flew it right through the

clouds. I then did a right hand spiral, and landed most rippingly in the middle of the flying ground. Well, this surprised the officers, and I think it more than surprised the instructor.

However, the afternoon came and I was told to go up first. The clouds were not very low in the afternoon, so I was able to get up high and still see land. So I went up to 1500 feet, put the nose down and did a left hand spiral, finishing up with a perfect landing. Of course, everyone came rushing up at once, expecting to hear me told off by the instructor, for spirals by pupils are not allowed. However, all he said was, 'In the future when you wish to try any tricks, get well clear of the flying ground, and for God's sake be careful.'

The chaps could not believe their ears, but this was not the end, for before I left the ground Captain Cox came up and told me next week I could have a flight in his 80hp machine.*

A brief note a week later gave warning to his family that he was about to move from Mousehold Heath:

Getting on fine, and shall be off to another camp next week. I had a ripping flight over Norwich, and did a spiral round the church tower.** I could just hear the bells ringing, but my engine drowned the sound. It was very nice over the town at 3,000 feet, so I had a good run.

Completing his instruction at Norwich, Ball was next posted to the RFC's Central Flying School at Upavon, Wiltshire, for the final phase of his training. He arrived there on December 19th 1915. It was hardly the best time of year to arrive at the CFS; just before Christmas, in the

* Probably a Bristol Scout single-seater.

** Norwich Cathedral.

depth of a particularly stormy, cold winter; and extremely isolated on the near-bald plains of Wiltshire. To add to his discomfort he was allotted a cold wooden hut bunk, with no heating, and due to the non-arrival of his personal kit in time, was even unable to seek solace in the officers' Mess. Illness in his family in Nottingham meant staying at Upavon over the festive Christmas season. Despite this catalogue of depression, Ball was kept busy with workshop theory and practice, lectures, and various routine duties.

As the new year opened he at last returned to his flying instruction. Weather conditions were bad, but Ball was now reaching the end of nearly eighteen months of constant endeavour to be sent to the fighting zone in France, and therefore flew whatever the conditions of the elements.

Almost straightaway he had yet another serious crash, which he described to his family:

> I was getting on fine up to Saturday morning, and was really thinking a lot of things, for I had got in front of the chaps in my Flight, and some of them have been here four months, trying to pass out. I was told to go off with a machine, and did so and landed quite all right. I was then told to go off again, I did so, and was thrown down 1,000 feet. The machine was smashed into matchwood. Oh and it was such a ripper. I would much rather have smashed myself than any part of the machine.
>
> However, as usual, I was not hurt at all. I came round in a few seconds and had not got a scratch, but I was so upset when I saw the machine. It was a bad day for everyone, for four other machines were smashed but only one pilot was really hurt, and he will not get over it. However, I must try to get over and have another smack…

This accident was in no way Ball's fault, but due to a high cross-wind as he was descending to land.

The CFS course, virtually a final 'polishing' period of training before successful pupils received their pilot's brevets, was relatively a short one, lasting for the average student between three and five weeks. Ball, very conscious that this was his last 'lap' towards his goal – France – remained at Upavon instead of taking the normal weekend leaves; preferring to spend the time in cramming his studies. On January 22nd he wrote to his parents:

> I have just come back from a cross-country flight. I had to make a forced landing for my machine went wrong. However, I managed to put it right, and with the help of the villagers at Colne, got off again. When I arrived back and handed in my report, my CO said that I was to go in for my Final, either this week or next, so I shall soon be

2nd Lt Ball after joining the NMDCC, prior to eventual transfer to the RFC

off. I shall visit home before I go, for it may be one or even two years before I get back again.

Three days later his father received a hasty note:

Am working now with full steam on, for my Final will be either tomorrow or Wednesday. Now I did not expect to pass through until next month, so naturally I have no cash for moving etc.

This was followed the next day by a brief telegram, 'Got Wings plus three days leave. Please wire £10.*

Albert Ball was officially transferred to the RFC with effect from January 29th 1916, and on the same date posted from Upavon to No 22 Squadron, RFC, stationed then at Gosport, Hampshire.

He actually arrived at Gosport on January 31st, and was immediately given duties as a flying instructor. His new duties were not any particular tribute to his flying skill, or indeed his ability to teach the art – he was still very much a new pilot. The need for instructors to be, ideally, men of reasonably long experience, with above average ability, and especially the peculiar aptitude for imparting their knowledge to the novitiate, had yet to be recognised by the British air services in 1915-16. Instead, any man wearing pilot's wings was considered capable of carrying out the duty, indeed, it was looked on simply as a duty, rather than the vocation it later became.

Flying Gosport's Avro 504 two-seaters and, occasionally, a Martinsyde, Ball worked hard at his new job, anxious to please, but hoping that he could very soon get away to an operational unit abroad. On February 6th, for example, a letter to Sedgley House told of, '… 30 officers up for instruction, and out of the 30, six off solo…' All within the space of one day's instructing.

---

* Official records give his 'Wings' award as from January 2nd 1916 – presumably an original typing error.

On February 15th he finally received official notification that he was posted to France, and on the 17th managed to scribble a brief farewell note to his family, before catching a cross-Channel steamer to Boulogne.

3

Baptism of Fire

O N arriving in France in the early hours of February
18th 1916, Albert Ball reported to the RFC Depot at
St Omer, and was immediately transported to join his first
unit, No 13 Squadron, which at the time was based
temporarily at Marieux. Equipped with BE2c and BE2d
aircraft, No 13 had originally flown to France on October
19th 1915; since then the unit had been employed on
general reconnaissance and army co-operation duties, the
latter including observation 'spotting' patrols for the
heavy guns of Royal Artillery formations in their
immediate battle area.

Ball arrived at a critical period in the fortunes of the
RFC. In June 1915 the German air services began
receiving the first examples of a new, single-seat
monoplane, the Fokker El. Though not a particularly
outstanding machine in terms of design or all-round
performance, the Fokker *Eindecker* possessed one great
advantage over its Allied opponents – a fixed LMG 08/15
machine gun, in front of the pilot's cockpit, capable of
firing 600 rounds per minute through the propeller arc. In
the hands of any relatively skilled pilot, the Fokker
presented an immediate threat to every Allied aircraft type
then in use in France; most of which were relatively slow,
poorly armed two-seaters. As the thin trickle of
Eindeckers reached the frontline units, they were initially
dispersed in ones or pairs to various German
reconnaissance units for protection duties. By the end of
1915 however, small groups of three or four Fokkers had
been banded into *Kampfeinsitzer Kommandos*, tiny
fighting units whose purpose was to seek and destroy, in
addition to their normal protection role. That they were

reasonably successful in their depredations of the Allied two-seaters was recognised by RFC higher authority, and on January 14th 1916, RFC Headquarters issued a statement of a new policy in air tactics:

Until the Royal Flying Corps are in possession of a machine as good as or better than the German Fokker, it seems that a change in the tactics employed becomes necessary... It must be laid down as a hard and fast rule that a machine proceeding on reconnaissance must be escorted by at least three other fighting machines. These machines must fly in close formation and a reconnaissance should not be continued if any of the machines becomes detached. This should apply to both short and distant reconnaissances. Aeroplanes proceeding on photographic duty any considerable distance east of the line should be similarly escorted... Flying in close formation must be practised by all pilots.

The crucial need for self-protection by RFC aircraft was due simply to the almost total lack of single-seat fighting aircraft at this time. The few Bristol Scouts available were allocated thinly in ones and twos among the squadrons, and these were merely armed in make-shift fashion, mostly by locally-invented modifications by offensively-minded individuals. The first squadron designated as a fighting unit, 11 Squadron, equipped with the two-seat Vickers FB5, had arrived in France on July 24th 1915, but had been virtually used as just another reconnaissance and general duties unit. It was not until the first week in February 1916 that the RFC's first single-seater fighter unit joined the war, when 24 Squadron, fully equipped with De Havilland 2 'pushers', arrived in France. On February 20th, No 20 Squadron brought a full complement of FE2b two-seaters to the fighting zone; and on March 1st, the second single-seater fighter unit came from England, No 27 Squadron, equipped with Martinsyde 6100 fighters. By the end of March a third fighter unit, No 29 Squadron (DH2s) also joined the BEF: The impact of these new, purely fighter squadrons was soon felt by the marauding Fokkers, and by April 1916 the 'Fokker Scourge' (as it had been referred to by overdramatic members of the British Parliament) was virtually abated.

The availability of the new fighters in increasing quantity, combined with the various lessons learned during the air battles between the German and French air services during the Battle of Verdun in February and March 1916, led to a completely new strategic policy being outlined by the commander of the RFC, Hugh Trenchard.

Henceforth Trenchard stipulated that only by offensive operations – 'leaning forward over Germany territory constantly' – could the true value of the RFC be accomplished. In pursuit of that dictum all single-seat aircraft were gradually withdrawn from the reconnaissance squadrons, and by the end of August 1916 all pure fighter squadrons were allotted separately to the various Army Wings, simply for fighting duties. This delineation of specific duties remained in force for the remainder of the war, and indeed virtually ever since in the world's air services.

To Albert Ball, fresh to the operational scene, and eager to commence his war flying, the machinations of senior commanders and high policies meant little. Settling in quickly with 13 Squadron, he took up BE2c 4352 on February 20th for thirty minutes' local flying; accustoming himself to the heavy machine he was expected to fly on operations.

On the following morning, piloting BE2c 4105, with a Lieutenant Green as his Observer in the front cockpit, Ball set out on his first-ever sortie across the German lines – and did not return to base that day!

Detailed for an artillery observation patrol, 'spotting' for the heavy guns, Ball's BE ran a gauntlet of anti-aircraft fire (known irreverently to the RFC as 'Archie'), and was then chased by no less than three Fokker *Eindeckers*.

Eventually his engine gave trouble and he was forced to land just behind the British lines, and spend a freezing night – there was heavy snow at this time before finally returning to base next morning.

For the next few days Ball flew only practice sorties locally, but on February 28th set out with Lt R Gregory* for another artillery registration patrol, which was completed without incident.

Members of No 13 Squadron, RFC at Savy airfield, 17th March 1916. (L-R): Woolf Joel (Ball's Observer), Ball, unknown, unknown, unknown, C E H Medhurst (later Air Marshal), unknown. Behind is Ball's BE2c, 4352

* Later, Major R Gregory MC, OC 66 Squadron when he was killed in a flying accident, Italy January 23rd 1918.

Next day Ball, in BE 4352, flew two sorties; another artillery 'shoot', and as 'fighting escort' to other BEs of the squadron. Again, nothing untoward occurred, though Ball's observer Gregory had to restrain Ball from leaving his 'charges' during the second sortie when Ball spotted a German aircraft in the vicinity and wanted to chase after it. The latter illustrated Ball's instinctive wish to get to immediate grips with an enemy, but also demonstrated the boy's immaturity in matters of air combat at this stage. It was certainly not in Ball's nature to desert his given responsibility as protector of his fellow squadron pilots and crews, but simply a natural reaction, acted upon immediately, by a boy of nineteen years, desperately anxious to prove himself in action.

The BE2c two-seater with which 13 Squadron was equipped was no fighting machine in terms of pure combat. Designed as an inherently stable aircraft, under-powered, and with only hastily-added armament comprising, usually, a single Lewis machine gun mounted on the front (observer's) cockpit; the BE was no real match for the more nimble Fokker monoplanes at this time roving the skies behind the battle front. Suitable only for its originally intended role as a stable reconnaissance vehicle, its built-in stability robbed its pilots of any real agility in manoeuvring should it ever become involved in aerial fighting.

Nevertheless, Ball regarded his various BEs as fighting machines, and seldom forsook any opportunity to use the unwieldy aircraft as offensive weapons. On March 7th, with Lieutenant Wolff Joel (son of the notorious Solly Joel) as his front-seat observer, Ball flew two patrols, in BE 4105 and 4352 respectively. Not content with his designated duties of reconnaissance, Ball rounded off each patrol by dropping down to strafe the German front-line trenches on his way back to base.

On March 12th the squadron moved en bloc to a different airfield, Izel le Hameau, but stayed there only a week before moving again, to Savy Aubigny aerodrome.

Here 13 Squadron remained for many months to come.

During the sojourn at Le Hameau Ball flew only one operational sortie – on March 16th, in BE 4352, with Lieutenant S A Villiers as observer – as fighting escort for a photographic mission by the squadron. At Savy, Ball and his fellow pilots were soon back at work, wasting no time in settling in to their new quarters. On March 19th, with Lieutenant Gregory, in BE 4352, Ball flew an artillery registration sortie in the morning. Next day he was again at the controls of 4352, this time with his closest friend, S A Villiers as observer. Taking off, the engine failed, and BE 4352 ploughed into the earth, wrecking itself in the process. Though both Ball and Villiers were trapped in the wreckage, they escaped without injury, and indeed were lucky that the BE had not caught fire. Undeterred by this near-miss with death, Ball took off in BE 4173, with Wolff Joel in the front seat, two hours later, and completed a successful artillery cooperation patrol.

Ball, as always, kept his family fully informed of his daily work and off-duty life, and therefore described his crash in BE2c 4352, in some detail. However, in his letters home on March 21st and 22nd, he ascribed the crash to being hit by anti-aircraft fire. The 13 Squadron records deny this, and it is puzzling that Ball should claim something which in fact did not occur. One of Ball's constant characteristics was undiluted honesty; and he was never known to lay claims for anything that was untrue, or even in any doubt. It is possible, though rather unlikely, that he had confused his thoughts here. On at least two previous occasions he had been forced to land a partly-crippled BE, stay with his aircraft overnight, and return to his squadron the following morning.

Although during his first few weeks with 13 Squadron Ball had several skirmishes with enemy aircraft during the course of routine patrol work, he had yet to actually engage a German opponent in straight combat. His first opportunity came on March 29th. Setting out in BE 4070, with his friend Villiers as passenger, Ball was due to carry out yet another artillery registration 'shoot'. In the event the cloud conditions nullified this intention. Between Vimy and Givenchy Ball's keen eyes spotted a German two-seater below and he promptly started to dive in attack. As Villiers rattled off one and a half drums of ammunition from his front Lewis at his target, the BE was 'jumped' by a second German coming down behind. Its fire smashed an engine bearer wire on the BE, but did no other damage, and both German aircraft dived away to safety on the German side of the lines.

Ball described the brief action in a letter to his father that evening, and ended the letter by saying, 'Please tell Cyril (his brother) that perhaps he had better stick to his regiment. I like this job, but nerves do not last long, and you soon want a rest.'

The reference to his brother, who had in the previous year followed Albert in joining the Sherwood Foresters (Notts and Derby Regiment), was to Cyril's expressed wish to transfer to the RFC.

More significant was this, his first reference to feeling the strain of constant operational flying. Since his first war sortie on February 21st, Albert Ball had completed 17 actual operational sorties, and had put in about an equal amount of practice and test flying locally around the unit's bases. During that period of seven weeks, he had been under heavy and accurate fire from anti-aircraft guns on each patrol, fought enemy aircraft, force-landed in damaged aircraft, crashed and written-off an aircraft – each adding to the mental stress of a boy already highly-strung by nature. On March 27th, flying BE 4200, with Lieutenant Gregory, on an artillery patrol, the aeroplane had its engine shattered by anti-aircraft fire, and Ball only just managed to put the machine down safely in some rough ground north-east of Aubigny. This, coming within less than a week from his near-fatal crash of March 20th, must have had some effect on Ball's nerves, but at this stage in his fighting career that effect was only slight.

With the resiliency of the young and fit, Ball soon got over his bout of depression. On April 1st he wrote: 'Oh, life is a rush out here... since my last letter to Dad, I have had three more fights, also a trip round the (gun) batteries with the major.* All took place yesterday. This makes four fights in one week.'

That same afternoon, with Gregory in BE 4200, Ball flew another artillery 'shoot' patrol, and over Gavrelle met and attacked an Albatros two-seater, though without visible result. For the next few days weather conditions of heavy rain, low clouds and high winds precluded operational flights, and Ball was only able to complete three patrols in nine days. On April 10th, with clearing skies, Ball took off with Villiers in BE 4200 on escort duty to a photographic patrol. On the return trip Ball (with Villiers' gleeful approval) broke away from the patrol as it reached the trench lines, and calmly attacked a German observation kite balloon. The *Drachen*, though well ringed by protective guns, was hastily hauled down – a moral victory for the audacious pair in their lumbering two-seater.

April 29th proved to be a red-letter day for Ball. With Villiers, in BE 4070, he set out at 5.15am for an early artillery shoot patrol. As he plodded back and forth over the trench system, registering and correcting the results of the gunners' shooting, a formation of five German aircraft approached the lonely BE2c. To Ball, odds meant little and he quickly nosed towards them – only to see the formation turn away.

Minutes later an Albatros CIII two-seater arrived on the scene and attacked. After only five shots from Villiers' Lewis gun, the German observer was seen to collapse in his cockpit, and the pilot immediately dived away to earth and safety, landing apparently undamaged south-east of Rouvroy. Typical of Ball's later combats, in this fight he

* Major A C E Marsh, OC 13 Squadron.

closed to within pointblank range of the Albatros – as he described in a letter home, '… the interesting point about it was that we could see the Huns' faces, and they could see ours, we were so near.'

Just after mid-day that day Ball achieved his ambition to fly a fast single seat scout. 13 Squadron had on charge a Bristol Scout, No 5316, and this was normally 'reserved' for use by experienced pilots only. After pestering his squadron commander for several weeks, Ball was at last considered worthy of a flight in the precious Scout, and he flew it for thirty minutes in the area of the aerodrome, revelling in the lightness of the Bristol's controls, its speed, and its manoeuvring agility. At 5.15pm that evening, he set out across the lines in the little Bristol, in the hope of finding any German aircraft to attack, but found none.

German kite observation balloon being "marched" to its ascent site

During the first week of May 1916, Ball continued his main operational work; flying BE2c's on artillery co-operation patrols, but on the 5th had another chance to operate by himself. His previous Bristol Scout, 5316, had been wrecked by another pilot, so Ball flew its replacement, No 5313.

This machine (like its predecessor) was armed with a machine gun, mounted on the fuselage, firing through the propeller arc and fitted with an early British gun interrupter gear. Ball took off at 6.30pm and crossed the lines, seeking a German opponent. Firing a few rounds from his gun to warm the mechanism – thus avoiding any freezing in the cold upper air – Ball continued his patrol without sighting any hostile aircraft, and returned to Savy airfield just before 6pm. On inspecting the Bristol afterwards he received a shock. The few rounds he had fired to 'clear' his gun had almost sawn his propeller in half, due to faulty timing of the gun interrupter gear!

As Ball put it in a letter home next day, '... if I had fired about six more shots I should have had to land in Hun land, for I could never have got back.'

At 3.45am on the morning of May 7th 1916, Ball flew his final patrol with 13 Squadron, when he piloted BE 2644 along the Avion-Givenchy road, looking for German troop movements, with Major A S W Dore as his passenger. His usual letter home that day was started with 13 Squadron, and completed after a busy and exciting day, with his new unit, 11 Squadron.

> Well, I have only got a few seconds in which to write this letter. At last my luck has gone a bit whonkey. I have received orders to go to No 11 (Squadron) and fly a new French machine, so this means the end of my leave. Oh, I am poo-poo, for I do so want a rest. However, it may be a great chance, so I will put a grin on and do what bit I can. The machine is one of the fastest going.

2.30pm – It is still raining, but I have got a machine to test at 4 o'clock. Yesterday at 5am one of our machines came down. Observer was killed at once, pilot was badly smashed about.

5.30pm – Oh! I am quite whonkey now. Have just been up to test my new machine. The new engine and undercarriage are now on. Well, I have never had such sport. I fooled about and banked it, having such a topping test ride. It is T T. So Huns, look out!

That morning, after his patrol with Dore, Ball walked across Savy airfield and reported to 11 Squadron, carrying a note from 13 Squadron's commander to Major T O'B Hubbard, commander of No 11, in which Ball was recommended for flying in single-seat Scouts. The 'new French machine' over which Ball had enthused in his letter was a Nieuport Scout, fitted with a 110hp Le Rhone rotary engine, and mounting a Lewis gun above the upper wing which fired ahead, out-side the propeller arc. It was Albert Ball's first meeting with the type of aircraft in which he was soon to establish himself as the RFC's leading fighting pilot.

His spell of duty with 13 Squadron had lasted 11 weeks without a break, during which time Ball had flown a total of at least 43 operational sorties, apart from many hours on test and practice flying. He was overdue for leave, and a temporary rest from the fighting, but medical acknowledgment of what, in a later war, became called 'battle fatigue' was not known in 1916. In any case, plans were already in being at the highest Army levels for an imminent massive land offensive by the end of June, and the British and Allied air services needed every 'fit' man they could muster in preparation for the forthcoming struggle.

Ball was philosophic about his delayed visit to his family:

Re-leave, I must say that although my nerves are quite good, I really do want a rest from all this work. I can stand a lot, but, really I have been coming on in leaps and bounds in the last few days, and it is just beginning to tell on me. I always feel tired... I have struck a topping lot of chaps in this squadron, and they look after me fine, but they all think me young and call me John. Well, this is no hardship, and I am very happy.

4

Emerging 'Ace'

No 11 Squadron RFC to which Ball had been transferred was already a veteran unit of the early aerial fighting over the Western Front. Formed originally at Netheravon on February 14th 1915, it was the first RFC squadron to be fully equipped with a single type of aeroplane, and with specific terms of reference as to its intended role. The machines were Vickers FB5 two-seat 'pusher' scouts, and the unit's role was designated as 'fighting duties.'

Joining the BEF in France on July 25th 1915, the unit was almost immediately in action, and by May 1916 had built up a high reputation for aggressiveness in combat; exemplified perhaps by the splendid fighting record of one of its Flight commanders, Captain Lionel W B Rees, who received a Military Cross for his prowess with 11, and in 1916, as commander of 32 Squadron, was awarded a Victoria Cross for his outstanding courage against great odds.

By May 1916, 11 Squadron was based at Savy Aubigny aerodrome, nine miles north-west of Arras, which it shared with 23 Squadron and Ball's former unit, 13 Squadron. Its commander was Major T O'Brien Hubbard, a veteran pilot who had obtained his pilot's certificate in 1912, and had been a Flight commander with 11 until recently.

In March 1916 the unit was ordered to select a few experienced pilots for eventual use in flying single-seat scouts, specifically the Bristol Scout and the new French Nieuport Scout; the first example of the latter, No 5173, being received by 11 on March 29th. The intention was to eventually form a Flight within the unit comprising solely scouts for fighting patrols and escort duties. Ball's previous experience in flying Bristol Scouts with 13 Squadron qualified him in this context, along with his obvious flair for such a role.

He duly reported to the 11 Squadron adjutant, Lieutenant A J Insall (brother of Second Lieutenant G S M Insall, VC, MC), bringing with him a note from Major Marsh which described Ball as, '... a keen and conscientious young man, and should do well.' Insall's impressions of Ball were, at first, of '... a bright young fellow, inclined to rather more self-confidence than the run of pilots of his flying hours... more self-assurance than his experience justified.'* On further acquaintance, however, Insall modified this judgment:

> For the first week or two he took things very quietly, prowled around on his own, wandered into sheds and watched engines being de-coked and aeroplanes re-rigged, smiled intelligently when spoken to, said little, and generally disappeared after working hours. He was a dark-haired youngster, with eyes to match, and on the rare occasions when I had conversation with him in his first fortnight, I was astonished to find so much serious thinking going on in such a youthful head, and such sensitiveness in one who had not come straight from school.

Ball took an immediate dislike to the shabby, unhygienic French house which had been allotted to him as his billet in Aubigny village, and resolved the situation with a piece of typical ingenuity, as he explained in his first letter home:

> No flying on account of rain. I have had my tent put on the job for it is placed on the aerodrome.

* *Observer* by A J Insall.

This will be nice for if ever a Hun comes I shall always be on the good work at once. One of our men is putting a wire round the tent, making a space of about forty square yards. This is being turned into a garden in which I hope to spend my spare time in the evenings. My work is rather a nerve pull, so I think it best for me to forget all about it after it is over.

For his kitchen garden, he requested his family to send him seeds for marrows, lettuce, carrots, mustard cress, cucumber, and sweet peas... 'and a few flowers.' By May 13th he gave a progress report on this venture:

I got up at 6am. It was raining so I could not fly. However, I got my tools out and set to work on my garden. In three hours I just managed to dig a piece of ground 12 feet by six feet, and in this I planted green peas... now my tent is full of chaps wishing to hear the gramophone.

Ball's bell tent (soon to be replaced by a home-built wood hut) was erected near the furthest aircraft shed on the airfield, some two miles from the squadron Mess. Insall's initial verdict of Ball being 'bumptious' for his age was only partly justified, inasmuch as Ball showed some outward signs of normal, youthful self-confidence. Yet Ball was never an extrovert; anything of a boastful nature was foreign to his character. Self-contained, often – mistakenly – taken to be of an introverted spirit, in fact Ball simply had little time for purely social facets in Service life. Friendly, if reserved, he enjoyed company, but never allowed it to interfere with his preoccupation with flying and fighting in the air.

Pure flying for the sake of it never attracted him; an aeroplane was simply his weapon of war, a vehicle in which to conquer his country's enemies. Apart from necessary air-testing between patrols, and after any maintenance, Ball rarely flew for simple enjoyment. His prime concern was always the efficiency of his aeroplane and its equipment, and the commonest view of Ball by his fellow pilots was of him tinkering with some aspect of his machine; or tending his plot of land. His new duties and the fresh surroundings gave Ball some relief from the strain he had been experiencing recently, but the ever-increasing toll of the air war soon had its effect on his temperament. Writing jointly to his sister Lois and brother Cyril on May 16th he explained,

> Do please excuse me not writing two letters, but really things are desperate just now, and my mind is full of poo-poo thoughts. I have just lost such a dear old pal, Captain Lucas. He was brought down by a Fokker last night about 5pm. Now don't show Mother and Dad this letter, and I will tell you about the fights.
>
> The Fokker came up behind the BE from the rear. It opened fire, and at once hit Captain Lucas, who was the observer. Lieutenant Wright was the pilot, and such a fine chap. He kept at his job, although he was hit in the shoulder. Fifty shots the Fokker fired, but Lieutenant Wright got over our side and landed, walked out a few yards and then fell down. Captain Lucas died in a few hours. The machine was brought back this morning, and I am not exaggerating when I saw it was soaked in blood, and full of bullet holes.* No 11, my squadron, lost six machines yesterday, and one

* Captain G B Lucas and Lieutenant F C A Wright, 13 Squadron

crashed today. Only one of our Flight is missing, and he was such a topping chap.*

Now for a bit of cheerful news. I was on patrol yesterday morning on my British scout.** I was at 12,000 feet and saw a Hun at 5,000. It started off and I went after it, catching it up when 20 miles over its own lines. It took 120 shots to do it in, but in the end it went down upside down. I got back but was Archied badly. In the afternoon I received orders to fly a new French machine. Did well on it, so they are now getting one for me. This means I shall be on one of the best machines England and France can give a pilot, so I hope for a good run.

Ball's combat was with an Albatros two-seater from *Kampfgeschwader* Nr 3 *Staffel* 17, which Ball first spotted over Givenchy and then chased towards Beaumont. He started his diving attack from some 2,000 feet above the German and kept up his firing until within a few yards of his target. His aim was accurate, wounding the German observer, and the Albatros was landed hurriedly near an army hospital at Hamblain-les-Pres. Though a clear 'victory', albeit not destroyed, the Albatros was credited to Ball as merely 'Driven Down'.

His reference to a new French machine was to the Nieuport 16 Scout, at least two examples being on 11 Squadron's charge – No 5173, which arrived at the unit on March 29th; and A126 which arrived on April 26th. Compared to previous aircraft he had flown, the Nieuport was far more agile in manoeuvre, and, for its time, fast in landing. Lightweight in structure, it proved to be rather delicate to handle for Ball initially, added to which the makeshift airfield at Savy did not make for smooth

* Second Lieutenant A M Mowatt, who crashed between two of the squadron's hangars, and later that day took off for a patrol and failed to return. He was later reported to have died of wounds on May 16th 1916 in German hands.

** Bristol Scout, possibly No 5326, which was then on charge of 11 Squadron.

landings, as witnessed on May 20th when Ball brought in A126 and promptly fractured the lower right main plane tip by bouncing on the undulating grass surface.

On May 22nd Ball was again over the German lines in his Bristol Scout, searching for enemy aircraft, and found a pair. Diving on an Albatros two-seater, his fire drove the Albatros down to land near Moyenneville. Ball next tackled an LUG reconnaissance machine, and again forced the German pilot to seek safety on the ground. Though both moral victories for Ball, each was credited as 'Driven Down'.

He was now given sole 'ownership' of a Nieuport Scout, 5173, and immediately spent many hours checking and improving the little scout to suit his individual taste. The main armament of the Nieuport comprised a single Lewis gun, mounted above the upper wing centre-section on a swivelling pillar-mount, which had a quick-release device worked by a Bowden cable enabling a pilot to tilt the gun back for changing drums of ammunition. On 11 Squadron this French-manufactured mounting was soon replaced by a simple, yet efficient curved, slotted rail which allowed the Lewis gun to be lowered to the pilot's eye-level. The gun could then be fired in an upward plane, or simply replaced in its former forward-firing, fixed position, firing above the propeller arc. The latter rail was devised by Sergeant R G Foster of 11 Squadron, and eventually became a standard fitment on British Nieuports and the later 1917–18 SE5 and SE5a scouts.

Two days after taking over the Nieuport, Ball landed from an evening patrol and was handed a leave warrant. Highly excited at the thought of seeing his home and family at last, Ball was shattered when Major Hubbard gently pointed out that the leave would have to wait a little longer. As Ball put it in a short note to his parents:

This put the stopper on all things for a few seconds, but after a second's thinking, I decided that it was only right that I should not go. It is hard work, but this comes about because I fly the Nieuport, and we have only two pilots who do fly it.

Burying his acute disappointment in work on his aeroplane, and in his garden, Ball gained satisfaction from a particularly successful day's fighting on May 29th. Setting out in Nieuport 5173 at 8am, he climbed gradually to 10,000 feet and started his search for enemy aircraft. Over Moyenneville he saw an LUG two-seater and promptly dived, closed with the German at 6,000 feet and fired half a drum at 30 yards range into the cream-coloured fuselage of his opponent. The LUG banked away violently and fell vertically, but Ball was unable to see its eventual fate as it merged with the earth below.

Continuing his patrol, Ball spotted three aircraft, an LUG escorted by two Fokkers, making towards Arras. Turning towards them Ball climbed and stalked the trio, waiting an opportunity to tackle a machine on its own. Soon two more Fokkers appeared, climbing above the original three enemy aircraft. Ball continued to wait. Then the LUG parted company with its escort, flying towards Oppy, and Ball attacked. Closing to 50 yards, he fired the remaining half-drum of ammunition into the two-seater, banked away to put a fresh drum on his Lewis, then bore in again. The LUG dropped its nose and dived to earth, its observer still firing from the rear cockpit, and putting eight bullets through the Nieuport. It eventually force-landed in open country, and Ball made for home, running a gauntlet of German anti-aircraft fire, which hit the tail of the Nieuport.

Just after 10am on June 1st Ball was airborne again in Nieuport 5173, and set course for Douai aerodrome where, at 10,000 feet, he calmly circled, waiting for any German aircraft to come up and offer combat. After nearly half an hour his patience was rewarded when he saw two machines – an Albatros CIII and a Fokker Scout – take off.

Diving on the Albatros, Ball commenced firing, but after only 10 rounds the two-seater dived hurriedly and landed back on its airfield. The Fokker meanwhile had worked round behind Ball and was rapidly closing in. Ball waited until it was within firing range and then, as the Fokker pilot opened fire, turned quickly and dived at the German. Again, he had only just commenced firing when his opponent dived to earth, landing in an open field, two miles west of Douai aerodrome.

Ball's conduct in these patrols contrasted greatly with his more usual tactics. Instead of plunging headlong onto any German sighted, he had shown restraint and patience; waiting the most favourable moment for attack when confronted with a total of five opponents on May 29th, and in permitting the Fokker to get within firing distance before evading and attacking in the latter combat. These were probably the only occasions when he displayed such restraint; in virtually all his future fights he was to simply attack on sight, regardless of odds or circumstances.

On June 10th Ball left France for his much-delayed leave, returning to 11 Squadron on the 23rd, feeling fresh and relaxed. In a letter just prior to his leave he had replied to his father's anxieties for his safety:

> Re – you saying that if anything happens to me... if anything did happen, as it quite easily may I expect you and wish you to take it well, for men tons better than I go in hundreds every day. However, I will be careful, as you wish, but I do like my job, and this is a great help.

That his parents' worries were justified was soon brought home to Ball shortly after his return to the squadron. On June 25th the fighter units of the RFC had been detailed for an all-out assault on the chain of German observation kite balloons just behind the German trenches. The final stages of preparation for the

impending land offensive along the Somme front meant
that these 'eyes' for the German artillery had to be put out
if there was to be any hope of surprise for the Allied
build-up in strength in the forward zones. In all, 23 kite
balloons were earmarked for destruction, of which 15
were actually attacked by RFC scouts. Ball, in Nieuport
5173, carried several 40lb phosphor bombs for the first
sortie, but failed to destroy the balloon he selected.

On his return he asked for permission to try again, and
at 4pm returned to the balloon line and successfully
destroyed a *Drachen*. Jinking his way through a hail of
anti-aircraft gun fire, his engine was hit badly and Ball flew
the eight miles back to the lines at only half-speed and at
tree-top height. One bullet taken from his scarred Nieuport
had ripped through the induction pipe, through an engine
bearer plate and penetrated three inches of wood. Ball sent
the bullet home – another souvenir of his personal war.

Two days later, on the 27th, as part of an internal
reorganisation of 11 Squadron, Ball with 2nd Lieutenants

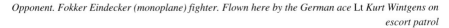

Opponent. Fokker Eindecker (monoplane) fighter. Flown here by the German ace Lt *Kurt Wintgens on
escort patrol*

Anderson and Griffiths, and Sergeant Reffell, were transferred to B Flight, which was in future to be the 'Scout Flight'. On the same day Ball had his closest brush with death to date. Flying Nieuport A134, he was detailed for a patrol at 7am. In his own words:

> I have only just missed being done in today... On my patrol I saw over the lines a lot of transport etc in a wood. I went over the lines to have a good look, but the old Huns did not like it. They surrounded us with shells from their Archie guns and at last we were hit. One of my cylinders was smashed off, also the machine got a few through it. One only just missed my leg. However, the engine stopped, but I saw what I went to see, and also managed to get my machine far enough over our lines to prevent the old fools from shelling it. Later on I had a new engine put in and the machine patched up, and it is now safely in the shed. I am sending half the cylinder to you.

On the morning of July 1st 1916, under a sunny, cloudless sky, 66,000 British troops spread along eighteen miles of shattered, muddy trenches on the Somme front were poised to attack. At a few seconds after 7.30am the first whistles were sounded, and the tide of khaki-clad men began to move forward – the first Battle of the Somme had commenced. Facing a murderous crossfire barrage of machine guns, the first wave lost 30,000 men, killed or wounded within one hour. By the end of the first day a total of 62,000 men had been slaughtered, mutilated or were just 'missing' – the bloody toll of twenty-four hours of war.

The British Army's loss in this single day exceeded the total battle casualties in the Crimean War, Boer War and Korean War combined. In the air the Royal Flying Corps had a total of nearly 200 aircraft in the battle zone, and these were directly opposed by some 130 German aircraft; the odds being heavily weighted in favour of the RFC. Nevertheless the RFC crews were stretched to their limits in attempting to cover and aid their comrades on the ground. Flying constantly throughout the day and into the night, they gave their utmost.

Ball, in a brief note to his mother that night, summed his day succinctly, 'I'm OK but oh so fagged. However I shall soon get over that. Things are on full steam just now, 2.30am to 9.30pm.'

On the following day Ball, flying Nieuport A134, accompanied four FEs across the lines at 10,000 feet, just after 5.30pm. He soon spotted a formation of six Roland CIIs coming towards the lines from the direction of Mercatel. As the two formations closed, the Rolands split up. Two of the FEs circled and returned to the lines, but the others joined Ball in attacking the Rolands. In the first clash, an FE sent one Roland spinning down to crash near the Mercatel-Arras road; whilst Ball dived on another Roland and hammered a full drum of ammunition into the side of its fuselage. The German fell away and crashed near its companion. Half an hour later, patrolling at 11,000 feet, he noticed an Aviatik two-seater over Lens. Stalking his prey, apparently unnoticed, Ball approached within 20 yards, jerked the firing cable of his Lewis gun, which jammed immediately! Diving quickly underneath the German, Ball let down the Lewis on its Foster rail, and fired nearly a full drum into the belly of the Aviatik. The two-seater fell sideways and hit the earth in a field; its wreckage strewn across a hundred yards of grass. This, the first occasion on which Ball employed his method of closing directly under an enemy and raking its fuselage from below at almost point-blank range, illustrated his lightning reaction to any change in circumstances during combat. It was a method of destruction he was to make peculiarly his own, and one which required steady nerves and cool courage.

His double victory on July 2nd provided him with his second and third officially confirmed victories, in the sense of enemy machines definitely destroyed and confirmed as such (counting his kite balloon victory of June 25th). Yet he was fully justified in saying, in a letter to his parents dated July 3rd, '… I now stand with six machines and one balloon to my credit.'

Since his first operational sortie in February 1916, Ball had destroyed for certain one kite balloon, and forced a second to descend; crashed two aircraft; sent two machines down out of control; forced three to land; and driven down two others. Using the term victory in its broader sense, Ball might have claimed a total of eleven by the close of July 2nd. That he chose only to acknowledge seven 'victims' as being, to the best of his knowledge and personal belief, victories illustrated his fundamental honesty and a natural reluctance to claim anything which was in any way doubtful in its conclusion.

This abhorrence of making any false claim was borne out by his next combat report, dated July 3rd. Flying Nieuport A134, his Lewis gun loaded with Buckingham incendiary bullets, and carrying eight Le Prieur rockets strapped to his interplane Vee-struts, Ball left Savy in the early afternoon on a specific mission – to destroy a kite balloon near Pelves. Crossing the lines at only 5,000 feet, Ball got within a quarter of a mile of his objective before the German ground crew saw him coming. They immediately started hauling the balloon down, but Ball dived to within 15 yards of the giant rubber 'sausage', fired his rockets, and released a stream of Buckingham ammunition into the bloated body of the balloon.

His rockets hissed past the target and exploded on the ground, but the bullets found their mark. As Ball pulled out of his flat dive, he realised that he had hit the balloon squarely, but it had not ignited, and on his return Ball was at pains to point out in his report that the balloon was hauled down, '… apparently uninjured.'

The first week in July 1916 quickly turned into a period of rain and winds 'dud', in the slang of the RFC – beginning on July 4th with a sudden downpour which flooded two of 11 Squadron's hangars. Unable to do more than local test flying, Ball took the opportunity to re-rig his Nieuport to suit his individual methods of fighting. His recent positive victory in which he had closed tightly underneath an enemy machine and fired his Lewis gun upwards convinced him that this was the surest way to destroy any hostile aircraft.

An accurate shot, Ball needed a steady gun to fire, thus requiring both hands to hold and fire the Lewis. As this meant releasing the control column, whether firing or merely changing ammunition drums, he needed the Nieuport to fly itself 'hands-off' during the crucial period of actual engagement. Accordingly he had the little biplane rigged tail-heavy. Typically, he made no mention of this to the other pilots on the squadron; it was a 'private' matter to Ball. Once the aircraft controls had been adjusted, and the re-rigging completed, Ball then had the Nieuport revarnished and generally smartened up in appearance.

The intensive flying of the previous few days during the initial stages of the Somme offensive, added to Ball's increasing fatigue, was taking its toll of the boy's nervous system. On July 6th he wrote to his father,

> Yesterday I was up at 5am and during the day had 12 flights, but at last Nature is asking to have its own way. However, I am not done yet, I shall get at them again soon.

In the same note he first mentioned his award of a Military Cross (MC). Ball was first notified of this award by the Wing headquarters on June 30th, and the following day Major Hubbard presented Ball with some MC ribbon to sew beneath his brevet.*

---

* The *London Gazette* citation was dated July 27th,1916.

BE2c, 4136, flown by Ball with No 8 Squadron, RFC, 1916

The award gratified Ball to some extent for the immense effort he had made in recent weeks, and his delight was akin to winning a prize for work well done. Nevertheless, his MC did not compensate for his mental and physical weariness, or the distress he felt acutely at the many familiar faces on the squadron which seemed to vanish abruptly each day. A letter to his sister on July 10th touched lightly on Squadron's losses:

> I am having a very poo-poo time, but most interesting. On the 6th three topping chaps went off and never returned. Yesterday four of my best pals went off,* and today one of our new chaps has gone over, so you can guess we are always having to get used to new faces...

* These four members of 11 Squadron were 2nd Lieutenants A E Spear and W A Wedgewood (both killed), H Floyd (died of wounds in captivity on July 11th 1916), and D H MacIntyre, a prisoner of war.

Another letter that day, to his father, revealed something of Ball's philosophy of air fighting.

I am feeling a poo-poo crock today. I went up this morning after Huns and managed to get underneath them, but could not get nearer than 3,000 feet owing to my engine. Am spending rest of the day trying to get it right. You ask me to 'let the devils have it' when I fight. Yes, I always let them have all I can but really I don't think them devils. I only scrap because it is my duty, but I do not think anything bad about the Hun. He is just a good chap with very little guts, trying to do his best. Nothing makes me feel more rotten than to see them go down, but you see it is either them or me, so I must do my best to make it a case of them.

His sentiments were shared by the majority of RFC pilots. Few men who actually did the fighting nurtured the artificial hate engendered by home-produced propaganda and 'armchair warriors' in England.

The bad weather continued to restrict operational flying during the second week of July, and Ball had to be content with a few minutes local flying, air-testing his aircraft. On the 16th he ferried Nieuport A133 to Candas Depot, and brought back another Nieuport, A117, as its replacement. By this date, B Flight, 11 Squadron possessed three Nieuports, two Bristol Scouts, two Vickers FB9s, and two of the recently-issued FE2bs – a motley mixture for the designated 'Scout Flight' of the unit.

That evening Ball, still desperately tired, quietly approached his squadron commander, Major Hubbard, and asked if it might be possible to have a few days' rest from the flying. Hubbard passed the request to Brigadier-General J F A Higgins. The result was not quite what Ball expected, as he explained to his father on July 18th:

The day before yesterday we had a big day. At night I was feeling very rotten, and my nerves were poo-poo. Naturally I cannot keep on for ever, so at night I went to see the CO, and asked him if I could have a short rest, and not fly for a few days. He said he would do his best. What has taken place has been that I have been sent to No 8 Squadron, back on to BE2cs. Oh, I am feeling in the dumps.

The decision to transfer Ball to an artillery co-operation and bombing unit came direct from Higgins, who probably realised that Ball was depressed and fatigued, but looked askance at such a request from a very junior subaltern. It is also possible that Ball's blunt out-spokenness on occasion, particularly in criticising some of the equipment and aircraft then in RFC use, did not endear him to higher authority. It has been suggested in past publications that Ball was exploiting his increasingly high reputation as a fighting pilot, and virtually demanding a rest as of right. Though Ball later acknowledged that he might have been slightly 'swell-headed' at that period, at no time did Ball attempt consciously to trade on his prowess or fame for personal gain in any way.

Major Hubbard, a gentle man by nature, was horrified by the response to Ball's request, and when Ball left 11 Squadron on July 17th to report to 8 Squadron at Bellevue airfield, Hubbard gave him a short letter to present to 8 Squadron's commander, Major P H L Playfair. In it Hubbard had written, 'You will find Ball a good little chap if managed in the right way. He is young, so naturally wants a little more rope than the older pilots.'

Hubbard then added a detailed list of Ball's fighting record to date, and ended by emphasising that if Ball felt like returning to 11 Squadron after a few weeks with No 8, Hubbard would be only too pleased to have him back.

5

Bombs, Balloons and Spies

O NCE he had accepted the fact of his removal from his beloved Nieuport Scout, Ball quickly readjusted to his 'demotion' to the cumbersome BE2s of 8 Squadron. Ball's highly-strung nature had always tended to alternate between high elation and low depressions and, with the boundless mental resilience of youth, it was not long before he was relatively happy and optimistic again. On July 20th he wrote to his parents:

Hello, all is well again, for I am well on the way to being OK. Last night Captain Parker came back from leave. He has got a Flight in this squadron. I asked him to get me in his Flight, and he did at once, so after all things are not so bad. I am advised to have my change here, and then ask to go back, stating at the same time that I have had enough rest. It is anything but a rest here, for the machines are so rotten and slow, but it will do me good. Yesterday I only did two flights, a patrol at 4am, and a bombing raid at 12pm, so perhaps it is the best thing. Well, I will not grumble, but will play up and get well again.

Ball had started his 'rest' in the early hours of July 19th by taking BE2c 2611 over the lines on a dawn recce of enemy gun positions, mainly to acquaint himself with his 'new' territory. At noon that day his was one of eight BEs from 8 Squadron which flew a bombing sortie against some railway sidings at Boyelles. Ball, again in BE 2611, carried no observer in order to compensate for his 'heavy' load of two 112lb bombs.

Undoubtedly the change from his recent lone fighting
to the orderly formation style of bombing and
reconnaissance began to calm his stretched nerves
quickly. There was now no driving urgency to be
constantly airborne, seeking German aircraft; only an
ordered routine of set sorties at specific times. The
consequent reduction in flying time gave Ball more time
for rest and diversion from his duties. Against this was the
accepted fact that the BE2c was a slow and highly
vulnerable machine for war operations; 'easy meat' for
any roving German scout, and virtually a sitting target for
anti-aircraft guns when over a target area.

Such odds against survival were not new to Ball and
therefore had no untoward effect on him, but the presence
of an observer bothered him. Always willing to take any
risk on his own account, Ball did not savour the
responsibility of another man's life being literally
dependent on him alone. For the various bombing sorties
he flew with 8 Squadron he (like the other pilots) never
carried an observer, but on artillery co-operation patrols
he had no choice in the matter.

Ball while serving with No 8 Squadron

On July 21st, piloting BE 1709, loaded with a pair of 112lb bombs but no observer, Ball was one of seven bombers led by Captain G A Parker to destroy a railway bridge over the canal at Aubigny-au-Bac. Two German scouts were seen at a distance but these made no attempt to interfere and the BEs returned unmolested. For the next few days Ball merely pottered around the airfield at Bellevue, having only a few brief local flights to air-test aircraft.

Writing home on July 25th, Ball announced:

> I am going back to my old squadron in a few days, but first I have promised to do a job, or at least try to do a job for the squadron. It is a rotten job, and one that has often been tried without success but, if God helps me in his usual way, I shall pull it off. I heard of it and asked for the job. The CO asked the General if I could do it, and at first he said, 'No', but yesterday he said I could try, so the first good chance I get the Ball will have another run. If this is successful I shall run slow for a time, as my nerves are not quite what they were.

The 'rotten job' which Ball had volunteered to do was to land an Allied spy behind German lines. The particular agent to be ferried across the lines, named simply as 'Monsieur Victor' in official records, had already made two attempts to complete the trip in one of 8 Squadron's BEs, but on both occasions, July 19th and 22nd, his pilot, Lieutenant A S R Clarke, had been unable to land due to heavy ground mists. In mid-1916 night flying in itself was a hazardous venture and few RFC pilots had much experience of it. Added to the normal risks, the possibility of actually landing in unknown territory behind enemy lines and successfully returning was problematical.

Ball, seeking an excuse to show higher authority that he was fit for fighting again, seized this opportunity to bring himself back in favour. Flying BE2c 4138, with the

The Happy Warrior. Ball wearing the ribbon of his Military Cross (MC), his first gallantry award

civilian agent and his paraphernalia stowed in its front cockpit, Ball left Bellevue at 8.15pm on the evening of July 28th. Just after crossing the trench lines the unarmed BE was attacked by three German scouts, but Ball managed to evade these and continued his flight deep into German-held territory as the gathering darkness closed in. The lone BE soon attracted the attentions of anti-aircraft gunners, who put up a fierce barrage, but the aircraft escaped without serious damage. Finally, Ball set the BE down in what appeared to be a deserted field.

To his dismay and no little annoyance, 'Victor' refused to leave his cockpit. Justifiably alarmed by the amount of attention already paid to the aeroplane by the Germans, the agent saw no point in continuing his mission that night. Furious at what he mistakenly judged to be sheer funk on the part of the spy, Ball took off again, made several more attempts to set the agent down – only to meet complete refusal by 'Victor' to disembark – and eventually flew back to Bellevue, landing just before 10pm. Though ostensibly unsuccessful, this unusual mission brought Ball personal congratulations from Brigadier-General Higgins the following day, with a message of thanks and praise from the RFC's commander Hugh Trenchard. More to the point for Ball was Higgins' personal assurance that he would soon return Ball to 11 Squadron.

Though looking forward eagerly to his promised re-posting to 11, in the meantime Ball continued to play his full part in 8 Squadron's daily routine. On July 30th, in BE2d 5799, he joined six other squadron aircraft in bombing the rail junction at St Leger. The seven BEs from 8 Squadron were part of a 30-aircraft raid and, when the leader was forced to retire early with engine trouble, Ball led the mass sortie to the target and back. On the following day, again in 5799, he participated in an evening raid on an ammunition dump at Corons. In the late afternoon of August 1st Ball took Second Lieutenant H E 'Tim' Hervey* as his observer in BE2d 2498 for an artillery 'shoot'; air-controlling the heavy guns of the 46th Division in an assault on the German rear lines.

Two more bombing sorties were flown by Ball on August 2nd, in BEs 2495 and 5876; an artillery registration 'shoot' in BE 1709 with Lieutenant A M Palmer on August 3rd; and five more sorties (four of these with Palmer) in the three days August 6th, 7th and 8th. One sortie was a bombing raid on a munitions dump at Boyelles, on which Ball flew BE2d 5876, and one of his four squadron companions for this sortie was a young New Zealand pilot later to achieve fame as a fighter pilot, Keith L Caldwell.**

On August 9th Ball took Tim Hervey with him in BE2d 5876 on a particularly audacious sortie. Ball had suggested to his Flight commander, Parker, that it would

* Later, Squadron Leader H E Hervey, MC, RMS, who became a fighter pilot with 60 Squadron RFC in 1917; was shot down April 8th 1917 in Nieuport Scout A311 and became a prisoner of war. He recounted his experiences in *Cage-Birds*, published 1940 by Penguin. After a flying career in Australia and England, Hervey rejoined the RAF in May 1940 and served throughout the Second World War.

** Now (1976) Air Commodore K L Caldwell, CBE, MC, DFC, who served with distinction in 60 Squadron in 1917 and in 1918 was OC 74 Squadron RAF.

be 'good sport' if the pair of them attacked a couple of German observation balloons. Parker agreed, received permission from Major Playfair, and at 11.30am both BEs took off for the lines. The action which followed is best described in Hervey's own words:

(L-R): Lt S A Villiers (one of Ball's Observers), Lt Cook (Wireless Officer, 13 Squadron) and Albert Ball. Taken at Savy Aubigny

We climbed to 4,000 feet and hung around until it was time to go. As soon as we poked our nose across No-Man's Land the ever-watchful anti-aircraft guns started up. I looked across the five miles or so between us and Parker's machine. It was easy to spot. Parker was lower than we were and making for his target, as always, like a bull at a gate. His machine was surrounded by the rather innocent-looking white puffs of shrapnel and by the very much more vicious and noisy black bursts of high explosives. Meanwhile the gunners were putting up a spectacular display around our machine. It had been hit a number of times by stray fragments but the damage was superficial.

We saw the balloon starting to descend and soon it was going down at an astonishing rate, swaying drunkenly under the pull of the winch cable. Ball started to dive and the next moments were a confused jumble of sights and sounds. Men running as we fired down on the balloon, machine-gunning from emplacements round the winch site, a glimpse of the balloon observer floating down by parachute, and an exploding shell knocking off a chunk of our port lower wingtip and fracturing a main spar.

Ball was yelling at me to keep my eyes skinned

for Huns as I switched the Lewis gun onto the rear mounting,* and we started for home. Fortunately the sky was empty of aircraft. We crossed low over the German trenches with a final burst of rifle and machine-gun fire from troops who doubtless had been eagerly waiting to join in the fun. As we passed over the lines there was a beautiful silence except for the pleasant sound of our RAF engine pounding away on all cylinders. We landed back at the aerodrome 55 minutes after take-off, and compared notes with Parker and Erskine (Parker's observer) while our ground crews crowded round inspecting two rather tatty aircraft.

Ball flew only one more operational sortie with 8 Squadron, a bombing raid on Beugny, flying BE 5876, on August 12th. One of seven aircraft from the squadron participating, he had the satisfaction of seeing his two 112-pounders fall squarely in the centre of the village. On the return trip he calmly attacked an Albatros two-seater which tried to harass the BEs and drove it down, though another BE pilot, De Courcy, reported this Albatros as 'diving steeply' after Ball's attack. That evening Ball air-tested a BE12, 6495, a single-seat 'fighter' version of the standard BE2c, and when later asked for his opinion of the machine – in view of his fighting experience – is reported as saying bluntly, 'It's like all BEs – bloody awful!' Like all aircraft Ball flew, he was never concerned with a machine's pure flying ability. If it did not fulfil his personal requirements for the fighting duties it was intended to fulfil, it was no use to Ball.

August 13th was spent in air-testing squadron BEs, and on the 14th – his 20th birthday – he received the finest 'present' he could have wished, when Major Hubbard of his old unit telephoned him to say he was to

* For this sortie Ball's BE had a rectangular hole cut in the fuselage floor, permitting Hervey to hand-fire his Lewis gun downwards and forwards.

Ball constructing his personal accommodation, Savy airfield, 1916

return to 11 Squadron, and that a new Nieuport Scout had
already been allocated for his personal use there. As Ball
wrote elatedly to his parents that day,

> You bet I shall be able to get my own back now.
> And won't it be OK to see my garden again? Do
> you know that if I had not been sent to this squadron
> I should have been a Flight (commander) by now
> and three pips? I think it has done me good being
> here, for I now know artillery work and bombing.
> All this helps to make a good flying officer.

The reference to his 'three pips' alluded to promotion
to Captain; Ball had been officially promoted to full
lieutenant, with seniority back-dated to August 1st 1916,
but at this time had yet to receive sanction to wear the
new rank. The minor grumble in this letter would appear
to have been simply a Parthian shot to his period of

'demotion' on 8 Squadron, because Ball often, privately, expressed little interest in rank or promotion for its own sake. The Army was simply a means to an end for Ball – to fight his country's enemies – and he had no ambitions for a military career.

On the evening of the 14th Ball took his kit and left Bellevue to travel to Savy aerodrome, where he moved back into the little wooden hut he had constructed just prior to leaving 11 Squadron four weeks before, with its adjacent kitchen garden and flower beds. During his absence, he had entrusted his garden to the care of a local civilian, and the little plot was now flourishing splendidly.

In the nearby wooden hangar stood a Nieuport Scout 16, A201, which had been received by 11 Squadron only twenty-four hours before, and which the gentle Hubbard had immediately allotted to Ball, on the return of 11 Squadron's 'prodigal son'.

Ball's contentment was complete – it had indeed been a happy birthday.

6

No Odds Too Great

Dearest people,

Hello, am back again in my dear old hut. All is OK, and my garden is fine. You will be surprised to hear that I have started with luck. I went up this morning and attacked five Hun machines. One I got and two I forced down. After this I had to run, for all my ammunition was used. However, I got back OK with only two hits on my machine. I have got one of the latest Nieuports and, oh, it is nice to be without a passenger again. I am on full steam again and hope to do tons of work. Please send as much stuff like tinned meats etc as you like, for I now have Mess on the aerodrome in my hut in order to be on the job all the time.

Ball in front of one of his Nieuport Scouts, with 60 Squadron, September 1916, and wearing the ribbons of his DSO, MC and Russian Order of St George

THIS note, written on August 16th, indicated with what eagerness Ball plunged back into his former routine of constant fighting and flying. As before he preferred to live alone, literally 'on the job', in his shanty hut next to the hangar housing his Nieuport Scout. To Ball he was in France for one purpose only – fighting. The off-duty social revels of his companions held little attraction for him, though he was no prude and made no criticism of his friends' attitudes to the business of war. Like most true individuals, Ball was content with his own company, but was usually friendly, if a little shy in the company of others. The mention of his starting 'with luck' referred to his first fighting patrol since his return to 11. Setting off in Nieuport A201 at 9.10am, Ball climbed to 8,000 feet over the lines, and almost immediately spotted four German two-seat reconnaissance aircraft, escorted by a Roland CII, all going south-eastwards over St Leger.

Selecting the Roland as his first target, Ball dived and fired a full drum into the German. The Roland banked away, circled, and then attacked Ball, who promptly closed to within 20 yards and fired a second drum into his opponent. The Roland fell away, its rear gun silent, and eventually force-landed south-east of St Leger. Meanwhile Ball had climbed to tackle the remaining four German machines, and he used his remaining two drums of ammunition in a series of short bursts and had the satisfaction of seeing two of the Germans put their noses down and dive away hastily, seeking safety.

Out of ammunition, Ball left the combat and returned to his airfield. Although he was personally convinced he had scored a victory over the Roland initially attacked, German records give no indication of any crash. His combat report was typically modest, and Wing headquarters finally credited Ball simply with two enemy aircraft 'Driven Down'.

On August 20th Ball notified his parents that he was temporarily a Flight commander, although in the same note he mentioned, 'I have been recommended for my second pip, but it is not through yet...', and he continued to sign his combat reports as Second Lieutenant. Rumours were rife in 11 Squadron that all scout pilots were to be amalgamated with 60 Squadron, and Ball expressed some slight anxiety about the possibility of having to leave his hut and garden yet again. On August 21st Ball flew a total of eight sorties, seeking German aircraft, but the few brief encounters he had were all inconclusive with his intended victims turning tail before he could get within firing range. Early next morning Ball was up again in A201, but throughout the morning and early afternoon continued to have no success in engaging an opponent.

At 7pm that evening Ball was acting as escort to a formation of FE2bs of 11 Squadron bound for targets in the Warlencourt valley, and crossed the lines at 5,000 feet. The bombers soon met opposition, and Ball saw a formation of seven Rolands south of Bapaume, heading towards his charges. Diving swiftly, Ball manoeuvred east of the Germans and then attacked the rear machine. As his Lewis gun commenced firing the Roland formation scattered wildly, but Ball's target was slow in reacting.

Closing to within fifteen yards, Ball fired again, emptying his drum of ammunition. Woken at last to his danger, the Roland rear gunner commenced firing as Ball turned away to change Lewis drums. With a fresh drum in position, Ball bore in again from the right side of the Roland, and after firing half a drum Ball watched the Roland side-slip, then fall vertically. As it neared the earth it turned on its side and in that attitude crashed close to a tiny village west of Bapaume.

Climbing back to the FE formation, Ball then saw five Rolands coming southwest over Vaux at 7,000 feet. With engine at full revolutions, Ball came up directly under the rear Roland of this formation, pulled his Lewis gun back on its Foster mounting, and at ten yards range fired a full drum into the fuselage just under the pilot's cockpit and

Opponent. Albatros D.1, 391/16 (Lt S.Büttner), an example of the type of enemy fighter Ball often met

engine housing. Still underneath the Roland, Ball changed Lewis drums and emptied a new one into the cream-coloured fuselage covering just above him. The Roland turned slowly, dropped one wing and fell straight down, its fuselage spewing grey smoke and crimson flames.

Three of the stricken Roland's companions then closed in on Ball, firing from front and rear guns. Ball rose to the level of the nearest German and hammered in a fresh drum of ammunition from only twenty feet range. The Roland, from *Kampfstaffel* 1, and piloted by *Offizierstellvertreter* Cymera, fell away out of control, with its observer, *Leutnant* Becker, dying in his rear cockpit. Falling 6,000 feet, the Roland wrecked itself on the roof of a house in a village.

Out of ammunition now, Ball was driven down to 2,000 feet by the remaining Rolands, but successfully evaded these and landed at Bellevue to replenish his ammunition drums. Refuelled and re-armed, Ball set out again to rejoin the FE2b formation, but soon ran into a trio of Rolands over Vaux. Closing the range to forty yards, Ball attacked each in turn and after a series of sharp combats all three Germans quit the combat and cleared east, leaving Ball as the moral victor.

By then the Nieuport was low on petrol and ammunition, so Ball turned for home. The little Nieuport had been hit eleven times by bullets, but these had caused only superficial damage in the fabric. The rest of this outstandingly successful sortie was described by Ball to his parents,

> This time my luck was not all on the spot. I was met by about 14 Huns, about 15 miles over their side. My windscreen was hit in four places, mirror broken, the spar of the left plane broken, also the engine ran out of petrol. But I had good sport and good luck, but only just, for I was brought down about one mile over our side. I slept near the machine and had it repaired during the night.

He had landed near Senlis, and after getting a message through to 11 Squadron to send a maintenance party, Ball, exhausted, simply slept on the ground next to his tattered Nieuport. Next morning, with the aircraft repaired sufficiently for a short flight, Ball flew A201 back to his airfield. The mention in his letter of a mirror being broken referred to a small convex car mirror which he had fixed to the centre-section cut-out of his Nieuport's upper wing, directly above his cockpit. This enabled him to see if any German aircraft was trying to get on his tail; an innovation which was later copied by many other RFC (and German) fighter pilots, and one which became almost standard modification on fighter aircraft of the 1939-45 war.

Ball's triple victory on August 22nd was destined to be his last with 11 Squadron. An extract from the personal diary of Sergeant W E G Crisford, the senior NCO in charge of B Flight, 11 Squadron's maintenance

Roland C.II ("Walfisch") two seater, a common opponent for Ball

crews, gives a hint of the esteem in which Ball was held at this time on the unit.

Lieutenant Ball is a very genuine fighter and jolly eager for an encounter with any Hun who cares to poke his nose anywhere within Lieutenant Ball's domain. Lieutenant Ball returned about 8.30am (Wednesday, August 23rd). Everyone was keen to inspect the machine, and when eyes were directed toward the windscreen it helped explain the nature of the scrap.

On his return to the squadron Ball was told that the recent rumours about a move to 60 Squadron were true, and that he was to report to the new unit that day, taking his Nieuport with him. 60 Squadron had just completed two weeks of recuperation and re-equipment at St André, having been withdrawn from frontline operations on August 3rd after a spell of appalling casualties.

On August 23rd, 60 Squadron, now designated as a Scout squadron, moved from St André-aux-Bois to Izel le Hameau, situated between St Pol and Arras, ten miles west of Arras and some two miles away from the nearest main road. The airfield, an immense level area with permanent accommodation for three squadrons located on the slopes leading down from the flying ground, was just south of Savy Aubigny. Later that day Ball, in his Nieuport A201, and Captain E L Foot, in Nieuport A187 gave 11 Squadron a brief aerobatic display before flying on to Izel le Hameau.

Commanding 60 Squadron was Major Robert R Smith-Barry, a veteran pilot of the RFC, a strict disciplinarian in certain aspects, and a man of outstanding and unusual talents. His name will always be associated with the Gosport School of flying training which he created and moulded to his own ideas on instructional methods in 1917-18, thereby pioneering a basis for flying instruction that has since become rock foundation of the world's flying training methods.

In Albert Ball, Smith-Barry recognised that rare quality, a born individual who did everything in his own individual way and was highly successful as a result. Accordingly, Smith-Barry allowed Ball free rein from the beginning, permitting him a form of roving commission which allowed Ball to continue his lone war.

On arrival at Izel le Hameau, Ball soon settled in, and retained his 'personal' Nieuport A201, being allotted his own ground crew comprising a fitter, Corporal Walter Bourne, and a rigger, Corporal J R Henderson initially.

On the following day Ball wasted little time in getting 'back to work', as he termed it, but flew only one sortie, during which he chased one German aircraft but failed to engage it. In the afternoon, Ball was visited by General Higgins, who jokingly remarked, 'I am putting your name

on a big board in the trenches in order to frighten the Huns.'
Twenty four hours later Ball was writing to his family:

> Today is the 25th, and I have again been in for it.
> Three fights. Two machines I brought down and one
> I crashed. Not so bad, four Huns in four days, is it?

In Nieuport A201, he had tackled a formation of
Roland CIIs and sent one down to crash, with two others
sent down 'out of control'. Of these, officialdom only
credited him with one Roland out of control.

During the next two days Ball spent most of the
daylight hours airborne, patrolling alone, well behind
German lines looking for hostile aircraft, but found none
with which he could engage in combat. On August 28th,
however, he had his busiest day to date. Still at the
controls of A201, Ball set out just after 9am on an
Offensive Patrol (OP) and surprised a pair of Roland CIIs
south-east of Bapaume.

Unseen by the German crews, Ball manoeuvred
underneath the nearest Roland and, with Lewis gun slanted
upwards, poured a complete drum of bullets into it at 20
yards, turned away to replace the empty drum, then
attacked again, firing half of the second drum. The Roland
fell in a steep dive, its pilot, *Leutnant* Joachim von Arnim,
dead at his controls, and its observer, *Leutnant* Böhne,
struggling manfully to gain control of the stricken machine.

As the aircraft came to earth Böhne finally succeeded
in setting the Roland down in a safe landing near
Transloy. Von Arnim had claimed his first air victory that
morning, and this sortie, his fourth for the day, had been
his last with *Fliegerabteilung* 207, *Kampfstaffel* 3, based
at Bertincourt, before his scheduled posting to the newly-
created élite *Jagdstaffel* 2 the following day.

Ball continued his patrol, but was on the return flight
before he spotted another two-seater over Bapaume.
Setting off in pursuit, he was forced to give up the chase

Hptm *Oswald Boelcke, commander of* Jagdstaffel 2

Jagdstaffel *2 line-up of Albatros D.1s, October 1916. In foreground (L-R):* Lt *Erwin Bohme, unknown,* Lt *Stephan Kirmaier, Max Müller*

over Beugny due to his dangerously low fuel state.

That same evening Ball, in A201, was acting as fighter escort for a formation of BEs and FEs of III Brigade intending to bomb a munitions dump at Loupart Wood. Setting out at 7pm, Ball crossed the lines just ahead of the lumbering bombers and sighted three German two-seaters over Bapaume, 3,000 feet below him.

In his normal tactic, Ball dived under the rearmost machine and fired a drum in crisp bursts along its fuselage belly. The German went down and forced-landed in a field north of Grevillers, apparently unharmed. Ball then dived on a Roland CII flying over the Cambrai-Bapaume road, got underneath it and fired a fresh drum in one long burst. Again his opponent went down and was seen to land near Beugny, without any visible harm.

Climbing back to 9,000 feet, Ball's keen eyes spotted four German two-seaters – two Rolands and two LVGs in loose formation south-east of Adinfer Wood. Diving straight through the middle of this formation, Ball saw them scatter and he fastened under the nearest Roland, firing a full drum into its engine and cockpit floors. The Roland spun away, but Ball, with two disappointments already, was determined to achieve a complete victory and accordingly followed his victim as it fell to earth. Closing to 20 yards range, Ball poured in another drum of bullets, and the Roland never came out of its dive; crashing nose-on just east of Ayette. It was the last of Ball's ammunition, so he set course for base.

August 30th proved to be a 'dud' flying day, with heavy rain during the morning, so Ball caught up with his correspondence, writing to Lois his sister.

You will be pleased to hear that I have now got more Huns to my credit than any English or French pilot. The Major asked for a list today, and it worked out:

Nieuport Scout, A201, 60 Squadron RFC in which Ball claimed sixteen of his victories. Note the (red) "spinner" (actually a fixed cone de penetration) and the cutaway upper centre-section

Another Nieuport flown by Ball with 60 Squadron, possibly A200?

84 combats.

11 Hun machines and one balloon brought down and seen to crash.

5 Hun machines brought down but not seen to crash.

12 forced down and damaged.

So it is not so bad, and I have done my best.

In a letter to his parents the previous day Ball had also touched on the question of his score, saying, '...They make it out to be 16 crashed in 84 fights, also the balloon, but I think it is only 12 crashed and the balloon out of 84 fights.' He then went on to say,

The Major had a long talk with me today. He is very pleased, and says I may have leave, next but one. Also I shall be coming home for a long rest soon, and I really think I shall get it. Oh won't it be

Le Prieur rockets attached to the wing struts of a Nieuport Scout

A1? I do so want to leave all this beastly killing for a time. Well, I expect to be in my dear old hut before long, for I think we are going to the old aerodrome.

In the late afternoon of August 31st Ball decided to 'beard the lion in his den' by a sortie to a German airfield, where he would wait for the German aircraft to come up to him. At 6.30pm, in A201, he set out for the lines, climbing steadily until he reached 11,000 feet, at which height he patrolled over Cambrai. Below him he saw twelve Rolands forming up over their own airfield, and immediately put the nose of his Nieuport straight down, plunging straight into the wheeling Rolands and forcing them to fly in all directions. Pulling the Nieuport out of its headlong dive, Ball climbed underneath one Roland, closed to 15 yards range, fired a long burst of 50 rounds into the ply-covered fuselage under the pilot's cockpit, and watched the Roland spin away drunkenly to crash just south-east of Cambrai.

Nieuport A126, 11 Squadron, in which Ball claimed two "victories" on 22nd May 1916

Turning to the remaining Germans, Ball jinked his way through the pack, firing whenever a target presented itself, and sending at least one Roland down fluttering, apparently out of control, which was seen to effect a rough landing in the narrow gap between two copses south-east of Bapaume. The vicious crossfire from the Rolands laced through Ball's Nieuport and one accurate burst slashed the Nieuport's engine ignition leads and the Le Rhone shuddered to a stop.

Out of ammunition and without engine power, Ball still refused to capitulate and drawing his Colt automatic pistol from its leather pocket inside his cockpit, he fired a clip of bullets at his antagonist. Gliding towards the lines, he crossed over the trenches through a hail of rifle and machine gun fire and finally landed safely at Colincamp. Once again, his all-out exertions had drained him, and he slept by his machine, returning to Izel le Hameau the following morning.

Nieuport A134, 11 Squadron, in which Ball was credited with three victories on July 2nd and July 3rd 1916

His return to base on September 1st was greeted with the news that he had been awarded his second gallantry decoration, the Distinguished Service Order (DSO). On the same day 60 Squadron moved its base from Izel le Hameau to Ball's old airfield at Savy Aubigny, thus bringing Ball back once more to his little hut and garden. Joyfully he settled in to the familiar surroundings, and that evening his happiness was completed when he was handed a warrant for a spell of home leave, effective from the next day.

The same day Brigadier-General J F A Higgins, commanding III Brigade RFC, issued an official summary of Albert Ball's fighting record to date. It read:

> Lieutenant Ball has had more than 25 combats since 16th May in a single-seater scout. Of these 13 have been against more than one hostile machine.

Nieuport A200, 60 Squadron, in which Ball claimed a victory on 15th September 1916

In particular, on 22nd August he attacked in succession formations of 7 and 5 machines in the same flight, on the 28th August, 4 and 10 in succession, on the 31st August, twelve. He has forced 20 German machines to land, of which 8 have been destroyed, one seen to be descending vertically with flames coming out of the fuselage, and 8 have been seen wrecked on the ground. During this period he has forced two hostile balloons down and destroyed one.

7

Hey-Day of a Fighter

WHEN Albert Ball returned to Nottingham for his leave he looked forward eagerly to seeing his family again, and planned to relax quietly, renewing acquaintance with old friends and simply enjoying himself in a modest way, fishing and generally winding-down from the previous hectic weeks of flying and fighting in France.

His rising fame had, however, preceded him. Local newspapers had been quick to exploit the news of his Military Cross award earlier, and had already added more column space to the exploits of this 20-year-old local 'lad' who had just been awarded a Distinguished Service Order; a decoration normally reserved for more mature recipients. In France too several journals and newspapers had spotlighted Ball's increasing prestige as a lone fighter of the air war, and other Allied countries' news media were beginning to note Ball's various activities.

As a result, when Ball arrived home, he found himself the centre of much attraction. He soon discovered that he was unable to take even a simple walk around his home city without being constantly stopped by local dignitaries and, more pleasantly if more embarrassingly, by an apparently endless stream of young ladies, each eager to meet this handsome young hero of the air.

Ball, though highly flattered, and privately delighted, by the adulation, was nevertheless acutely shy of such public homage. Like any young, healthy boy, he savoured the attentions of the opposite sex, but felt distinctly and genuinely uncomfortable when praised to his face by the many older men who approached him on the street. His presence was very much in demand by local social matrons, but as far as possible Ball declined such invitations as gracefully as he could. He preferred the company of his loving family, particularly his beloved mother, and sister Lois, to any formal social gathering.

Home on leave, 5th October 1916. Ball posing with the sons of the photographer, Charles Shaw, Sedgley House

The admiration of Ball was not restricted to a hero-hungry public at this time. Within the Royal Flying Corps his prowess and fighting methods had brought him many venerating admirers. The late Air Vice-Marshal Stanley Vincent, who in 1916 was a contemporary of Ball in 60 Squadron, said of him:

> He was a quiet introspective little chap, and not exactly 'friendly' with anyone in particular. We were all billetted in the local village but not Ball who had a small hut on the aerodrome near his Nieuport. There he lived in solitary state with his violin and little garden – so much so that we called him the 'Lonely Testicle, or Pill'. He had a red spinner on his propeller and was the only one of us so 'decorated', but the Huns obviously soon got to know it! When he went on leave at this time I flew his aeroplane while mine was being patched up, or having an engine change, and during that week I couldn't get near a Hun! As soon as they saw the red spinner they dived away east. I felt very brave but had no success at all.

Another 60 Squadron fellow-pilot was the late Air Chief Marshal Sir Roderic Hill, then a junior Lieutenant, who said of Ball:

> He used to sit in his hut on the aerodrome and, with the help of his gramophone, hatch out his schemes. He had but one idea; that was to kill as many Huns as possible, and he gave effect to it with a swiftness and certainty that seemed to most of us uncanny. He nearly always went out alone; in fact he would not let anyone fly with him, and was intolerant of proffered assistance.
>
> To surprise his enemy he made clever use of the Lewis gun mounting on the Nieuport scout. There was a curved rail down which the gun had to be run

to change drums. By exerting pressure on one side of the stock of the gun, he held it rigid when nearly down and pointing upwards at about 80-degrees.

By skilful manoeuvre – and incidentally by pluck and determination – he was able to zoom up beneath his intended victim; then, by a slight oscillation of the control stick to cause his gun to rake the target fore and aft, at a range of 30 feet or so. So astute was he at reaching the underneath position that he flew most of the way to Cambrai just underneath one of our Moranes, quite unsuspected by its pilot. I found that my own efforts to emulate Ball in reaching a favourable position beneath a Hun so irritated it that a melee ensued in which I soon lost any idea of what was its 'underneath' and what was its 'top'.

To say that Ball fought with his head is almost superfluous. He was evidently the offspring of a vixen and a lion. He would sight a formation of as many as twelve Huns afar off, would rise into the sun, fly above them and fire off a burst or two. This would invariably shake the formation's nerve and cause it to open slightly. One pilot, a little more nervous or less disciplined than the rest, would lose his station. In a flash Ball would be on him, and almost as soon the deadly shooting would send him up in flames.

Ball's security lay in the fact that he fought at such close range that the rest of the hostile formation dare not fire at him for fear of hitting its own aeroplane. The moral effect of his attacks was so great, and such fear did the sight of the red spinner carried on his propeller boss create, that during one period the Huns would not attack him. Figuratively speaking, Ball did the work of a whole squadron by himself.

Souvenir. The famed red "spinner"
of his Nieuport Scout

Souvenir. Propeller from Nieuport Scout 5137,
5th October 1916

The red spinner of which Vincent and Hill spoke had been presented to Ball just after his posting to 60 Squadron by Air Mechanic Charles Simpkin,* and was probably an old Morane 'Bullet' spinner, refurbished and doped bright red by Simpkin. Ball was delighted with this personal 'fighting mark', and used the spinner on many of his Nieuports, particularly A201, whilst with 60 Squadron. (He revived the habit in 1917 after his posting to 56 Squadron, as noted in a later chapter.) This, his first such spinner, he brought home with him in October 1916, and it was mounted in the hall of the family home later. Such was the fame of the spinner that Roderic Hill featured it in the 1916 Christmas card he designed for the squadron, depicting a line of 60's Nieuports at dawn.**

A contemporary of Ball in 11 Squadron was Lieutenant (later, Wing Commander) William Fry, MC, who joined the unit towards the end of July 1916. He described his impressions of Ball in his autobiography:***

> It was at this time that I first met Albert Ball. Foot was taking me round and introducing me to the other pilots. Ball was standing outside his canvas living-hut near the hangars; around it he had laid out a small flower garden where he spent a lot of his spare time. No one could say he was welcoming or forthcoming, he was briefly polite and then carried on with what he was doing. All the same he was bound to make an immediate impression on anyone. He was short and slight, beautifully proportioned, with black hair, dark eyes

* Simpkin was later personal mechanic to Captain W A Bishop, VC, DSO, MC, of 60 Squadron, and similarly made a spinner for Bishop's Nieuport B1566, doped blue. Air Marshal William Avery – 'Billy' – Bishop, VC, CB, DSO, MC, DFC, died peacefully in his sleep on September 11th 1956.

** Strictly speaking, this 'spinner' was a *cone de penetration*, ie a fixed item, but was usually termed 'spinner' by RFC pilots.

*** *Air of Battle*, W M Fry.

and a rosy complexion almost of the kind one would associate with a girl.

Withdrawn and not sociable in the Mess, he would escape to his hut as soon as he could, where he could sometimes be heard practising his violin. He always played his piece in squadron concerts and even now I can remember that his usual contribution was the old stand-by 'Humoresque'. He was a skilled self-taught fighter pilot well before most of us had gathered much idea what it was all about... most of us were still at the stage of learning to fly and grow accustomed to be in the air.

Ball was utterly fearless and uncommunicative. Though he was considered somewhat unfriendly, he was never unpopular and did not make unkind remarks to or about anyone. Unexpectedly sensitive, he was nonetheless a self-effacing, skilled and dedicated killer with no other motive than to use his machine and armament to shoot down enemy aeroplanes. There was in his attitude none of that sporting element which to a certain extent formed the basis of many scout pilots' approach to air fighting. Ball never made jokes about it. In the nature of things he was bound to be killed sooner or later as he always looked for and never refused a fight.

Keith L Caldwell, a New Zealander who later gained great distinction in the RFC and RAF as a fighter pilot and fighting leader, originally joined 8 Squadron for his 'baptism' of operational flying, at the same period that Ball was 'rested' with the unit. His opinion of Ball and, particularly, his methods is of especial interest and was one shared by many other notable fighter pilots:

Ball was not very long in No 8, but with adjoining tents in the orchard at Bellevue, just across from 8's aerodrome, I did get to know him as much as one could in that short spell. I remember he was pretty upset at being sent over to us to BE2cs from his Nieuport, but we understood that he had become a bit 'difficult' to handle, and his coming to us was in the way of a calming down process at the orders of the Brigade CO, General Higgins.

Ball had been doing a lot of flying, many hours a day, and probably badly needed a rest. He would have got this respite with us as our artillery observation role etc on slow old BE2cs would lack much of the excitement he was used to.

The 1916 summer was a lovely, fine, warm one and some of us would gather outside Ball's tent, where he played his gramophone in the long evenings. He was a hero to us, with his successes in many air fights, and he looked the part too; young, alert, ruddy complexion, dark hair and eyes. He was supposed to be a 'loner', but we found him to be friendly. One feels now, looking back, that he would have lacked the balanced capacity for planning or employing strategy in the air, as did Mannock* and McCudden** to name two who did. I, for one, was not surprised to hear the sad news of his going 'missing' from a 56 Squadron patrol later. One felt that it could only be a matter of time before he 'bought it', as he was shot about so often.

Caldwell's comment on Ball's 'lacking' in matters of air fighting strategy is succinct. In early and mid-1916 the few fighter pilots of the RFC had no precedents to learn from in the arena of aerial combat. Tactics and strategy were empirical, and each man perforce learned his 'trade' in the only way available – by dint of hard-won personal experience. A few individuals had previously set isolated

* Major Edward Mannock, VC, DSO, MC.

** Major James Thomas Byford McCudden, VC, DSO, MC, MM.

Ball being driven by his sister, Lois, October 1916

Thoroughly at home with any mechanical vehicle, Ball in an Oldsmobile in Nottingham, late 1916

yet splendid examples of dogged courage, but in general
the young single-seater pilots like Albert Ball had to
invent their own methods. Ball's personal tactics owed
nothing to any previous example. Only by his individual
experience in fighting German aircraft had he gradually
evolved his unique mode of tactical evaluation. Though
rightly regarded as an outstanding pioneer in fighting
tactics in the 1914-18 air war, Ball employed little
cunning or preconceived planning in his methods.

His simple fighting creed had a parallel with another
contemporary, Major Lanoe Hawker, vc, dso, who, when
commanding 24 Squadron RFC in mid-1916, pinned on his
squadron notice board one brief operational 'order' to his
pilots, 'Attack everything.' In all this Ball was completely a
man of his time; a period in the air war when individual
prowess and outstanding courage were the mark of the
successful fighter pilot. Only in late 1916 did the first
examples of air strategical thinking first begin to emerge,

Ball with the family pet collie, "Goff", at home

Ball and his mother

and these came chiefly from the German air services in France when the first German fighting *Jagdstaffeln* commenced operations against the RFC and the French.

By early 1917, when Ball returned to the fighting after many months in England, the tenor of aerial

Ball taking delivery of a three-wheel Morgan car at Colmore Depot

conflict had changed drastically; the days of the lone fighter were virtually over. Safety and success lay in teamwork, and the inheritors of the example set by Albert Ball had evolved into fighting leaders; men who thought in terms of numbers, stratagems, pre-planned tactical and strategic advantage.

On his return from leave to 60 Squadron on September 11th, Ball was given command of A Flight, though the usual corollary of promotion to Captain had yet to be authorised. On the 13th he received a telegram notification from Wing headquarters of the award of a Bar to his DSO; and two days later was officially notified that he had been awarded the Russian Order of St George, 4th Class. The official award of this latter decoration was made on September 24th, on which date Ball wrote home, pinning a scrap of the pale orange and black ribbon to his note.

Congratulations on his awards poured into the squadron, and Ball was now firmly established as the RFC's leading fighter pilot. As always, Ball accepted these honours with modesty, but privately was elated by his recognition. His delight was innocent of conceit; he merely looked upon his various decorations as official 'rewards' for his work, akin to prizes awarded after a college sports event in which he had been first among the competitors. They also provided him much satisfaction on behalf of his family. Throughout his life Ball sought the approval and good opinion of his father, and constantly hoped to be a credit to his mother, whom he loved deeply and unwaveringly. In his respect for and adoration of his mother, Ball hoped that the public adulation and recognition would reflect some of its honour upon her.

Ball's return to France coincided with a significant change in the air war. Along the Somme front the German air services had been increased in overall strength by withdrawing certain units from the bloody Verdun struggle, and by the end of August 1916 the German 1st and 2nd Armies facing the British along the Somme could muster an air strength of 35 flying units, plus a total of about 60 fighter aeroplanes distributed loosely among a number of *Kampfeinsitzer Kommandos* – single-seat scouts in small formations.

In September this overall strength was increased to 69 units including, significantly, two freshly-formed *Jagdstaffeln* – exclusively fighting squadrons equipped with the very latest single-seat scouts available. Of these the most prominent was *Jagdstaffeln* 2, commanded by the leading German fighter pilot then, *Hauptmann* Oswald Boelcke. This squadron first assembled at Bertincourt airfield, about halfway between Peronne and Cambrai, on August 27th, though on that date it possessed no aircraft.

On September 1st the first aeroplane arrived, an Albatros DI flown in by *Vizefeldwebel* Rudolf Reimann, which was joined the same day by two Fokker DIIIs ferried from a nearby aircraft park. Yet another new arrival on this date was a young cavalry officer, Manfred *Freiherr* von Richthofen – destined to become Germany's 'Ace of Aces' of World War One.

During the following two weeks the *Staffel* was brought up to operational strength, and on September 16th six new Albatros DIs were delivered to Bertincourt. That same evening *Leutnant* Walter Höhne flew his DI to the lines and claimed an FE2b two-seater as his victim. On September 22nd *Jagdstaffel* 2 moved from Bertincourt to Lagnicourt airfield, and continued to take a steadily increasing toll of its British opponents.

The Albatros DI biplane, with which *Jasta* 2 was mainly equipped, was a streamlined, semi-monocoque fighter, with a fuselage covered in plywood in place of the more usual fabric coverings of the period. Powered by a 150 or 160hp Mercedes engine, and armed with two fixed LMG 08 machine guns on its forward fuselage geared to fire through the propeller arc, the DI was the most powerful and heavily-armed fighter on the Western Front in September 1916. It was to be the progenitor not only of successive, improved Albatros designs, but of virtually every main fighter design produced by all countries participating in the conflict. It would be no exaggeration to claim that the Albatros DI set a pattern for fighter design for nearly twenty years in nearly every country's air services. Though less agile in manoeuvrability than its chief Allied opponent the Nieuport 16 Scout, the Albatros was faster, stronger and twice as well armed.

As a Flight commander, Ball often led other pilots of the squadron on combined patrols, bomber escorts, or specific missions, but whenever occasion permitted he continued to fly his lone patrols over the German lines, searching for German aircraft. On September 15th the third phase of the Somme battles was instigated, when a total of 49 land tanks accompanied the infantry across the shell-torn mud in yet another onslaught on the firmly held German trenches.

In order to preserve some element of surprise for these new weapons, an all-out aerial attack was ordered for the 15th against the line of German observation balloons. Of the 23 balloons earmarked for destruction, eight were designated as targets for 60 Squadron's pilots, and the RFC's commander, Hugh Trenchard, visited 60 to ask for volunteers for the mission.

Ball, in Nieuport A200, accompanied by Second Lieutenant A M Walters, took off just before 10am, bound for the German *Drachen*. As 'anti-balloon' armament each Nieuport carried a battery of eight Le Prieur rockets, attached in two batches of four, to the interplane vee-struts, ignitable by electric contact switch. On arrival at their objective both pilots were dismayed to see that the balloons they had been detailed to attack had been hauled down.

Climbing to 4,000 feet, Ball saw some German aircraft below him, north-east of Bapaume, and dived on a single-seat biplane, followed dutifully by Walters. When within 200 yards Ball fired all eight of his rockets in one hissing salvo, but missed the target. Closing to within fifty yards of the thoroughly startled German, Ball then fired half a drum from his Lewis into his opponent's tail section. The German machine at once spun wildly down and crashed east of Beugny. Meanwhile Walters had better luck with his rockets, firing these in salvo at an LUG two-seater and seeing one rocket smash into the fuselage of the German machine. Within seconds the LUG was ablaze and the burning wreck fell near Bapaume.

At 3pm Ball was airborne again, this time in Nieuport A212, and patrolled over Bapaume at 7,000 feet. Spotting an Albatros two-seater going east over the town, Ball approached it with the sun's glare behind him and got to within 50 yards before firing a full drum of ball and Buckingham bullets into his prey. Releasing the Lewis gun on its rail in order to replenish it with a fresh drum, Ball was hit on the head by the gun as it tilted back and momentarily stunned. By the time he had regained control his opponent had gone to earth.

Unbeknown to Ball, it was a machine from *Fliegerabteilung* 221, based at Ruyalcourt, and Ball's bullets had found their mark, wounding its observer, *Leutnant* von Wurmb in the left forearm, and forcing its pilot to land hastily at Nurlu.

Two hours later Ball took off in Nieuport A201, intent on attacking the German balloon line again, and therefore once more carrying eight Le Prieur rockets on the aircraft outer struts. At 3,000 feet he noticed three Roland CII's in formation over Bapaume and could not resist the temptation to tackle them.

Diving onto the trio, he fired all eight rockets first and, as he anticipated, the Rolands broke formation immediately in confusion. Fastening under the belly of one Roland, Ball lowered his Lewis gun and raked it at 20 yards with a full drum of ammunition. The Roland skidded sideways – its crew from *Kampfstaffel* 13, *Oberleutnant* du Cornu and *Unteroffizier* Carstens both seriously wounded – then tumbled down completely out of control to crash into some rough ground northeast of Bertincourt. Du Cornu, grievously wounded and injured in the crash, succumbed to his injuries two days later.

Ball's use of three different Nieuports in the course of a single day's fighting was unusual in his own case, though not uncommon amongst most of the other pilots of the squadron. Few pilots in the RFC had the privilege of 'owning' a particular aircraft for their sole use; whilst the normal turnover of machines due to attrition, necessary maintenance, or simply circumstance, meant that it was exceptional for any pilot to fly a particular machine for any appreciable length of operational service.

In Ball's case however he continued to be privileged in being allocated his own aircraft, and when a new Nieuport, A213, arrived on 60 Squadron on September 16th, Ball promptly took it for his personal steed. Having his red spinner mounted on its propeller boss, the rigging set for tail-heavy flying characteristics, and its cockpit re-arranged to suit his taste – including a leather 'holster' for the personal Colt automatic pistol he invariably carried on sorties – Ball then spent several hours getting the upper-wing Lewis gun harmonised to his favoured killing range of 60 feet, and testing its accuracy on a ground target butt. Although in command of a Flight, Ball had yet to receive authority to wear the third 'pip' of a Captain and continued to sign all reports as Lieutenant DSO, MC.

On the 16th another new arrival to 60 Squadron was Captain Ernest Leslie Foot, who replaced Captain A S M Summers* as B Flight commander. Foot had been a close friend of Ball's on 11 Squadron, and on the 18th both men, flying rocket-equipped Nieuports, were detailed by Major Smith-Barry for an anti-balloon patrol with a difference. Hearing of 13 German balloons being in operation near Bapaume, Smith-Barry told Ball and Foot to patrol over the balloons but *not* to attack, unless in exceptional circumstances.

* Killed in action, flying Nieuport A136, on September 15th, 1916, during a balloon attack.

Both men set out at 11am, and within 20 minutes ten of the offending *Drachen* had been swiftly hauled down to relative safety. The remaining three had probably been left aloft as deliberate decoys to entice the Nieuports down within anti-aircraft range, but Ball and Foot stuck to their strict orders and ignored these.

Despite the obvious success of this bluff patrol, Smith-Barry received a diplomatic 'wrist-slap' from his Wing commander next day, for 'poaching' on other squadrons' duties and 'preserves'...

Ball's next combat of note came on the 19th when, flying A213 on an evening OP, he dived from 7,000 feet to 2,000 to attack an Albatros two-seater east of Adinfer Wood, fired a drum at 50 yards range, and watched the German flee nose-down towards St Leger. Closing again to 25 yards, Ball fired a second drum and the Albatros made a hasty forced landing in a field south-east of St Leger. Scrupulous as ever in his claims, Ball reported the machine as landing 'all right'.

On September 21st came a triple 'victory'. Much impressed with the shock effect of using Le Prieur rockets against aircraft in his recent combats, Ball set out in A213 with a full load of rockets on a fighting patrol, seeking aircraft. At 6,000 feet near Bapaume he found a formation of six single-seat scouts just north of the town. Diving to their level of 2,000 feet Ball repeated his tactics of September 15th by first firing a salvo of all rockets and then, as the German formation scattered frantically to avoid a fiery death, fastening under the nearest scout and blasting a full drum of ammunition into its belly.

The German dropped its nose sharply and made an erratic landing near a railway line below. Sliding quickly under a second hostile machine, Ball slammed two drums in swift succession into this target. The German scout fell into an uncontrolled sideslip and crashed alongside its companion.

Turning for home Ball was set upon by the remaining

four Germans, eager for vengeance. They continued to snipe at the Nieuport as it approached the lines, and Ball used his remaining ammunition in warding off the attacks, crossed the lines and landed at Savy.

With fuel and ammunition replenished Ball set out again at 5.15pm and climbed quickly to 7,000 feet. Over Bucquoy he saw a pair of Roland CIIs about 3,000 feet below him, and immediately dived, closing to within 20 yards of the nearest's tail and firing a full drum into its fish-like fuselage. As he did so, he was joined by another roving RFC scout (either an FE8 or a DH2, according to Ball's combat report), and the Rolands dived away east to relative safety. Five minutes later Ball spotted the same pair of Rolands returning, dived at them and fired two drums at the first from 30 yards. This Roland started slowly spinning to earth, and Ball turned his attention to its companion, getting off one more drum at a fleeing target without apparent result.

Letting it go, Ball searched the ground below for sign of his first opponent and soon saw its wreckage strewn across a hedgerow. In a long dive to 500 feet Ball then fired two full drums into the wreckage, in his own words, '… to make certain of the passengers.'

The finale to this combat, in which Ball had deliberately fired nearly a hundred rounds into the wreckage of his victim, displayed an entirely uncharacteristic 'blood-lust' on his part. Though never a devotee of the 'gentlemanly' attitude to his opponents professed by many of his contemporaries, and therefore not concerned with any particularly chivalrous approach to his job of killing as many of his country's enemies as possible, Ball, like a majority of fliers of his period, was almost always impersonal to his victims. His attitude to opposing aircraft was similar in many ways to that of his German 'opposite number' at that time, Oswald Boelcke, leader of the elite *Jagdstaffeln* 2. Boelcke expressed his own feelings on the subject of victories in a letter to his father:

Mother will be saying again that it is not right to number our victims in this unfeeling way. But we don't really do it – we do not number our victims who have fallen, but the machines we have brought down. That you can see from the fact that it only counts as one victory when two inmates are killed, but that it still remains a 'number' when both inmates escape unhurt. We have nothing against the individual; we only fight to prevent him flying against us. So when we have eliminated an enemy force, we are pleased and book it as one up to us.*

That Ball had introduced a 'personal' element into this particular combat was almost certainly an indication of the high pitch to which his nervous reaction to his work was now reaching. During his few remaining days with 60 Squadron he was airborne at every possible opportunity, seeking out and destroying.

Ball was well aware of his heightening inner tension, as witnessed by the fact that he quietly approached his squadron commander, Smith-Barry, and bluntly told him that he (Ball) was in need of a rest. Smith-Barry, surprised at this idea, queried his reasons for thinking so, and Ball said quite simply that he knew his nerves were failing because he was taking unnecessary and foolhardy chances of late.

---

* *Knight of Germany*, Professor J Werner.

8

Loner

THOUGH Ball was fully aware of the increasing tautness in his 'nerves', he displayed no outward sign of it during his few remaining days with 60 Squadron. The insatiable urge to be constantly flying and seeking opponents continued unabated.

On Friday, September 22nd, in Nieuport A213, he set out at 11.30am as fighting escort for a small bombing formation. At 7,000 feet he spotted two Roland CIIs over Bapaume, and was joined in his attacking dive by an FE2b from 11 Squadron. At 50 yards Ball fired two drums into one Roland, which immediately made for safety and landed in open ground south-east of Bapaume. The other Roland fled east.

At 4.40pm Ball was airborne again in A213, searching the clouds at 5,000 feet east of Bapaume. After nearly an hour of fruitless patrolling a solitary Fokker DIII single-seat biplane suddenly emerged from a cloudbank, its pilot blissfully unaware of the Nieuport above him. Ball manoeuvred behind the Fokker, shallow-dived, and then crept up still unobserved to a position 15 yards under it. With his Lewis gun slanted upwards at an acute angle, Ball fired one drum in one long burst directly through the floor of the Fokker's cockpit, swiftly changed drums, and awaited results; his trigger finger crooked around the gun trip.

The Fokker gently turned and, its nose slowly dropping, fell away in a half side-slip through the clouds. Ball did not follow his victim, but in his report later stated that because he had used Buckingham tracer-incendiary ammunition, most of which was distinctly seen entering the pilot's cockpit, he thought it most likely destroyed. In fact, his victim was *Leutnant* Winand Grafe from *Jagdstaffel* 2, whose Fokker plummeted into the ground one kilometre east of Bapaume.

Continuing his patrol, Ball climbed to 12,000 feet and noticed two Roland CII's coming south towards Bapaume. Closing to within 50 yards of the nearest he fired a full drum into it, then attempted to get underneath its tail to deliver the coup de grace. The Roland's crew, Corporal Karl Kohn and *Flieger* Albert Reichl, chose discretion as the better part of valour and headed east in the fastest possible dive, leaving Ball far behind.

After several fruitless sorties the following day, Ball took off in A213 in the early evening, hunting above the Bapaume-Cambrai road area. He was carrying some of the recently-issued 'double' drums of ammunition which each contained nearly 100 rounds, in place of the older drums of just over 50 rounds at most.

Rittmeister Manfred von Richthofen (centre) with his pilots of Jagdstaffel *11, the "Red Baron's" first command*

Ball soon found his quarry when he saw four Rolands approaching from the direction of Bapaume, and started a diving attack. The Rolands sheered away but Ball then found himself running head-on into a loose gaggle of Albatros two-seaters which had been trailing the Rolands. Spraying a drum in the general direction of this second batch, Ball pulled down his Lewis to reload, but the unaccustomed weight of the new type of ammunition drum caused him to fumble his usual smooth action, and the fresh drum slipped from his hand and fell inside the cockpit, jamming his rudder control wires.

Momentarily out of control the Nieuport yawed and then flew straight through the Albatros pack. As he became the target for each rear gunner's fire, Ball frantically retrieved the offending drum, fixed it in position on his Lewis, and took swift stock of his situation. Seeing one Albatros on his own level flying alongside, Ball swerved and came up under it.

Firing a full drum from only 15 yards range, Ball watched his bullets stitch a ragged line along the Albatros' fuselage from tail to nose. The two-seater veered crazily, lifted one wing, and fell away pluming smoke and flames as it spun to earth outside Bapaume. Ball turned for the lines, his ammunition exhausted, followed by the rest of the Albatros formation. Whenever a German approached too close for comfort, Ball turned and feinted an attack, at which the antagonist retreated. Crossing over the trenches, Ball brought his tattered Nieuport in to land at Savy, where his mechanics counted 13 bullet holes in the fuselage, some close to the cockpit.

On September 25th Ball met a particularly tough German two-seater crew. Just after noon he had taken off in A213, ostensibly for an attack on hostile kite balloons, though he carried no rockets on this sortie. At 7,000 feet above Bucquoy he noticed an Albatros heading towards the Allied lines. Chasing after it, Ball attempted to secure his usual under-firing position. The German crew must have been too experienced to allow this because every attempt by Ball was foiled by skilful manoeuvring on the part of the German pilot. For the next 30 minutes the duellists turned and manoeuvred, each firing brief bursts as the opportunity arose, but without success. As Ball described the combat in a letter home:

> We kept on firing until we had used up all our ammunition. There was nothing more to be done after that, so we both burst out laughing. We couldn't help it – it was so ridiculous. We flew side by side laughing at each other for a few seconds, and then we waved adieu to each other and went off. He was a real sport that Hun.

Recounting this flight to a news reporter later in his home town, Ball added the sincere rider, 'I should have been sorry had I killed him, and I think he would have been sorry too had he finished me off.'

Ball was quite mistaken in his assessment of this fight and its outcome. The German crew comprised *Flieger* Tewes (pilot) and *Leutnant* Martin Hoffman, from *Fliegerabeilung* A237, based at Vendhuille. Hoffmann, the observer, had been killed by Ball's deadly accurate fire, whilst Tewes was seriously wounded. Ball's interpretation of Tewes' hand-waving was probably a product of his personal reaction to such an unusually extended combat, whereas it is much more likely that Tewes was simply trying to indicate the parlous state of himself and his observer. Undoubtedly, if Ball had been carrying more ammunition he would have had a relatively simple task in securing a complete victory on this occasion. As Oswald Boelcke had said, 'victims' did not count on a 'score' – only machines.

On this date (25th) Ball first signed his combat reports as Captain. As he wrote home:

> This is the address I meant to get before I finish

and now I have got it, and I don't care how soon the war ends. But I hope it won't be long.

The following day Ball flew A213 on an evening OP, setting off at 6pm and climbing to 11,000 feet for his patrol, rather higher than his accustomed fighting ceiling. He soon noticed four German two-seaters flying towards Sapignies – two Roland CIIs and two Albatros. Ball dived, but the German crews had seen his approach and set off at top speed. Overhauling the rearmost machine Ball managed to sink half a drum into its fuselage, saw its observer collapse in his cockpit, either dead or wounded, before the machine dived earthwards. To Ball it appeared to be quite under control and he reported it as such, making no claim for any victory.

The 27th proved to be unfruitful despite several hours of flying and searching the sky, but the next day saw him further increase his tally. In A213 he crossed the lines at only 2,000 feet in the later afternoon, heading for the German observation balloon sites near Haplincourt. Though not detailed for a balloon strafe – indeed, Wing headquarters had forbidden such attacks except on specific occasions – Ball hoped to use a *Drachen* as 'live bait', hoping that an attack would bring up defending aircraft for combat. His hopes were realised as he made his first pass at the balloon. Hurrying up towards him were three Albatros two-seaters.

Banking quickly away from the balloon, Ball manoeuvred underneath the first Albatros, slid back his Lewis, and poured nearly 100 Buckingham tracers into it at 15 yards range. The German spun viciously and crashed in a field outside Haplincourt. Ball turned for home, his mission accomplished.

Half an hour after landing Ball was airborne again in A213, this time accompanied by his friend and fellow Flight commander, Leslie Foot, who was flying a new French scout, a Spad S7, A253. Over Bapaume the sky was busy with several German formations at various levels. Selecting one mixed bunch of five Roland and Albatros two-seaters, Ball and Foot dived to 2,000 feet in attack. Foot's victim seemed to wilt under his fire, turned over and spun into the ground. Ball's target too went to earth but appeared to be under control.

Climbing back to 7,000 feet Ball then attacked another batch of Germans coming southwards towards Bapaume. Rising close under the nearest he fired a full drum and the German pilot immediately put his machine's nose down and landed. With his remaining ammunition Ball forced two German machines away from the tail of a British machine, and then flew back to Savy.

Of the two aircraft Ball had sent down to land, apparently under control, one is identified as crewed by *Unteroffizier* Schedler (pilot), who was severely wounded, and his observer *Leutnant* Walter, from *Fliegerabteilung* 238, based at nearby Lagnicourt at that date. In a brief letter home that evening Ball wrote, 'Got my 28th, and Foot his third.'

Rain and mist prevented any worthwhile flying on the 29th, but on the last day of September Ball added success to success in the course of a day of almost continuous combat. His usual Nieuport A213 was undergoing an engine change in its hangar, so just before 11am, Ball took off in his old favourite Nieuport A201. He was one of six Nieuports and two Moranes despatched by 60 Squadron which joined with some FE2bs of 11 Squadron to provide a strong fighter escort for eleven BEs from 12 and 13 Squadrons intending to bomb Lagnicourt airfield, the home of *Jagdstaffel* 2 and other German flying units. The FEs joined them prior to crossing the lines, flying at 7,000 feet.

Nearing the target Ball noticed an Albatros two-seater some 2,000 feet below, dived and commenced firing, but the German turned eastwards and fled. As he turned Ball saw a second Albatros two-seater immediately above him. He pulled down his Lewis and fired just five rounds of Buckingham, after which the Albatros tumbled sideways, a roaring furnace of flames and oily smoke. Ball described the end of the Albatros in an interview some weeks later:

> She was a two-seater and I fired five rounds into her. She burst into flames and fell upside down. Although she dropped like a stone, I saw her observer climb out of his seat and jump clear of the flames. He must have preferred that kind of death to the chance of being roasted.

At the moment Ball fired at this machine an FE2b of 11 Squadron, crewed by Second Lieutenant E P Roberts and Lieutenant Collins, also claimed to have hit the Albatros. Although RFC Headquarters afterwards officially shared this victory by crediting both Ball and the FE crew, two other 60 Squadron pilots in the fight, A D Bell-Irving and A M Walters, both independently

Studio portrait of Ball, sold widely as postcards

reported Ball as its actual conqueror. This victim of Ball has, in the past, been consistently identified as an Albatros D Scout of *Jagdstaffel* 2, piloted by *Leutnant* Ernst Diener. Though indeed Diener died in action on this date, all Ball's combats throughout the day were with German two-seater machines.

Relaxing outside his hut at mid-day, Ball noticed a concentration of anti-aircraft bursts attempting to bring down a German reconnaissance aircraft north of Savy, ran to his Nieuport A201 and immediately took off in pursuit. As the German turned towards Vimy, Ball managed to get within 30 yards and fire half a drum, but the Albatros put down its nose and out-paced the Nieuport. Frustrated, Ball returned to Savy.

That evening, once more at the controls of A213, Ball took off at 6pm for an OP over the Bapaume-Graincourt-Cambrai zone, flying at 12,000 feet. His attention was drawn by anti-aircraft bursts to a formation of eight Roland CIIs over Bapaume, which turned towards Cambrai as he approached. Catching up over Graincourt, Ball got under one Roland and at 15 yards fired a full drum of Buckingham between the pilot's seat and engine housing. The Roland started down, apparently out of control, and Ball changed drums and fired a further half-drum at the falling machine.

Before he could follow it down, Ball was attacked by a second Roland, preventing him seeing the result of his attack, and in his report he simply wrote that he thought it must have crashed. Continuing his patrol, Ball was surprised when the same formation of Rolands appeared again some minutes later, approaching Bapaume from the direction of Cambrai. Diving quickly, he fastened underneath the closest Roland, fired half a drum at pointblank range, and then fired the rest of the drum into it as the Roland began to fall away to earth.

Again he was prevented from seeing the conclusion of his onslaught by the close attentions of a second German, and was forced to break off the fight due to lack of ammunition and return to Savy.

The following day, October 1st, proved to be Albert Ball's final day of combat for the year. He was awake early and just after 7am, in response to a telephone call from an anti-aircraft battery, took off in A213 to look for reported hostile aircraft on the British side of the lines. Finding none, he flew across the lines towards Bapaume and then circled above the German airfield at Lagnicourt, deliberately inviting opposition. Within minutes three single-seat biplanes, which Ball mistakenly identified as 'Roland single-seaters',* could be seen climbing to engage him.

Ball dropped quickly on the nearest and fired half a drum at 30 yards from a half-rear position. He was then at merely 500 feet height and saw his opponent make a hurried forced landing. The other two cleared east. Climbing back to 8,000 feet Ball continued his hunt, and next saw an Albatros two-seater, painted in an overall brown dope, over the outskirts of Hamelincourt, some 4,000 feet below.

As the Nieuport arrived above the German, Ball dipped its nose and fired a full drum of Buckingham tracers, which he distinctly saw tear through the fuselage of the Albatros. With the German observer firing what Ball described as 'explosive bullets' at him, the Albatros dived and shakily landed, though Ball was unable to see whether it actually crashed.

Flying towards the lines, he met an all-white Albatros and manoeuvred under its tail. Canting his Lewis gun upwards, Ball started firing, only to have a gun jam after the first 50 rounds. As he attempted to rectify the gun, the white Albatros went down to land in a large field near Hamelincourt. With little fuel in his tank, and a useless Lewis gun, Ball set course for his own airfield.

* These were almost certainly either Fokker DIIIs or Albatros Ds; Roland single-seaters did not reach the front-line units until a later date.

Back at Savy Ball was greeted by Major Smith-Barry with the news that he was to be sent home to England soon; firstly for a spell of leave, and then to a posting in the Home Establishment. Ball was overjoyed, not only because of a rest from flying and killing, but for the opportunity to be with his family again. He was now recognised as the leading fighter pilot of the British air services, and his fame had spread to all levels of the Allied forces.

On October 3rd he was interviewed by his Army commander, then Brigadier-General Higgins, and afterwards had luncheon with his former 8 Squadron commander, now his Wing commander, Lt-Colonel P H L 'Pip' Playfair. Each congratulated him profusely on his outstanding fighting record. Ball, though naturally flattered, was deeply embarrassed by such an overt display of 'gratitude' from his elders, and modestly brushed it all aside in his brief note to his family informing them of his imminent homecoming.

Returning to Savy he finished packing his kit, and presented his well-used gramophone and records to his Flight ground crews in token of his personal appreciation for their long hours of devoted labour. In the squadron Mess that evening he was, in the standing tradition, 'dined out' by his fellow pilots on 60 Squadron and several crews from neighbouring squadrons.

Blushing crimson at the various tributes spoken, Ball was thankful to slip away reasonably early in the proceedings and escape to his little hut before the celebrations became too hectic. Next morning, having made his personal farewells to Smith-Barry and his close friend Leslie Foot, Ball started his journey by road, rail and ship to England.

As the acknowledged leading fighter pilot of the Royal Flying Corps on that date, Albert Ball's combat record for 1916 was indeed prodigious. Such acclaim was based solely on the official summary of his many achievements and therefore, necessarily, incomplete in the context of

Ball (far right in leather coat) walks away from a bad landing in Bristol Scout, D5554 while serving with No 34(R) Squadron at Orfordness

complete historical accuracy. The contemporary knowledge of RFC Headquarters could only be a cautious official record, lacking, for obvious reasons, any knowledge of the conclusion of many combats on the German side of the lines.

With the enormous advantage of hindsight, the past availability of German records, official and private, and the accumulated outcome of patient, objective research by a number of dedicated historians over the intervening years; it is now possible to give, at least, a more accurate assessment of Ball's 1916 record of combat.

From February 18th to October 3rd inclusive, Ball had actually been engaged in a total of 58 known individual combats* – sometimes several in the course

---

* The official reference to Ball's contemporary record dated August 30th 1916 quoted a total of '84 fights' to that date. In fact, research has shown that this was simply a reference to his total operational sorties not all of which included any fighting.

of a single patrol – including attacks on kite balloons. The known results show that Ball had definitely destroyed 17 aircraft and balloons; forced a further 20 to land in varying states of damage and crew casualties; sent five aircraft down completely out of control; and driven down a further nine. This 'tally' was achieved in a total of merely six months actual operational flying, including his many weeks of plodding daily over the lines in the obsolete BE2cs of 13 and 8 Squadrons.

Possibly more important, however, was Ball's splendid example of Hugh Trenchard's intended policy for the RFC of a constant offensive in the air. In an era when individual pilots were only just beginning to frame the basic 'rules' of aerial fighting, Albert Ball had by his personal example and self-taught expertise shown the way to success, and thereby set a standard of sheer courage and the will to win for all others to aspire to and emulate. As Brigadier-General J F A Higgins has recorded:

> When Ball started his career the casualties among the British airmen exceeded those among the Germans by very considerable numbers. There can be no doubt that sooner or later this state of affairs must have been disastrous. The encouragement given to the whole force by Ball's startling series of successes cannot, in my opinion, be overestimated.*

* *Albert Ball*, vc, dso, R H Kiernan.

9

Home Establishment

WHEN Ball arrived at Nottingham railway station on the morning of October 5th, he was met by his sister Lois and driven to the family home, Sedgley House; there to be greeted not only by his parents but by a crowd of local news reporters and photographers. As a prominent 'local hero' Albert Ball was front-page copy, and his arrival in England was recorded and illustrated in all local and no few national newspapers and journals.

By midday the news of his homecoming had spread widely, and Sedgley House became the focal point for a host of visitors, telephone calls and messages of congratulation. A Nottingham photographer, Charles Shaw, had already been engaged to come to Sedgley House that afternoon, and he spent several hours photographing Ball, his family, and even the pet collie, 'Goff'; photographs which were quickly reproduced in hundreds of papers and magazines worldwide.

Ball bore this adulation with smiling modesty. He was overjoyed to be reunited with his family, and privately relieved to be away from the incessant flying, fighting and killing in France. He now hoped for a quiet, relaxing leave, pottering in his garden shed, doing a little fishing, and visiting friends and acquaintances. His hope was in vain, and the two weeks flashed by in a kaleidoscope of social invitations, constant pestering by well-meaning admirers, and a flood of congratulatory letters, telegrams and messages.

Among other civic recognition was a formal luncheon with the mayor and aldermen of the city, and when called upon to reply to the mayor's flowery eulogy, Ball, red with embarrassment, could only mumble that he was pleased to have done his duty by his family and his home town.

In an effort to obtain some privacy Ball took to wearing a plain Service raincoat over his bemedalled uniform, when strolling around Nottingham, but this proved of little avail and he continued to be recognised and approached by people wherever he went. On October 8th he was interviewed by a local news reporter who questioned him about his methods of fighting in the air.

Ball replied, 'To bring down a lot of Huns you have to be patient and practically live in the air. There are not many of them about and you have to be quick and seize your chance or the bird will have flown away. Sometimes you make 10 flights a day and never get a fight. Often it is in the early hours of the morning, when it is cold and you don't feel very keen on going up, that you get your chance. On a few occasions I haven't had time to put my clothes on and I have gone up in my pyjamas. It was jolly cold, I can tell you, and unfortunately I have never brought down a Hun when clad like this… altogether I have been brought down six times myself, generally with my engine smashed up. Always I have been lucky enough to land in my own lines; once quite close to the Sherwood Foresters, my old regiment, in which I enlisted as a private.'

Despite a crowded social calendar, Ball made time to visit his old engineering works in Castle Boulevard, and spent a happy day talking with the staff and discussing the firm's increasing prosperity. He also gave priority to visiting the families of several airmen and officers he had known in France, to reassure them of their relatives' safety and circumstances. To Ball, whose family was his greatest love, such visits were far more important than attending the social fripperies being pressed upon him from every quarter.

On October 18th Ball reported for duty with 34 (Reserve) Squadron at Orfordness, on the east coast. Nominally he was posted there as a fighting instructor, thereby – at least, in theory – to pass on to embryo pilots

Family group of Ball, his parents and sister Lois and the collie "Goff", 5th October 1916

the benefit of his experiences in France. On paper this appointment was no doubt logical to the posting authorities in the War Office. The state of the 'art' of flying instruction in the RFC at that period was still very much piecemeal. Flying instructors were, in the main, men being officially 'rested' from a tour of operational fighting, and thus, in the minds of the RFC headquarters staff, ideal men to pass on their firsthand knowledge of aerial fighting to student crews.

Ball and his proud parents, 5th October 1916

(L-R): Albert Ball, Lois Ball's current boyfriend and Cyril Ball

Such a policy failed to take into account two important facets in instructional technique. A good instructor is almost invariably born, not 'made', with the necessary ability and enthusiasm for his subject to be able to impart his knowledge fully to another. Equally, ex-operational pilots, particularly highly sensitive men like Albert Ball, needed time to readjust from the nerve-stretching daily fighting in France to a calm routine of a training syllabus. The fairly crude state of all flying instruction in 1916 held no attractions for the great majority of ex-operational pilots. Having lived with the ever-present probabilities of death in a variety of horrifying forms, they looked askance at the prospect of trusting their necks to the highly doubtful capabilities of raw 'Huns' – the universal RFC soubriquet for any student air crews – especially in the slow, ancient types of flying machines then in use at all flying schools.

At Orfordness Ball soon found that his working routine was undemanding; an occasional flight in a Bristol Scout or Avro 504 demonstrating some basic aspect of air fighting, or simply air-testing the machine. On the morning following his arrival he was honoured by the Prime Minister, Lloyd George, and his daughter, by being invited to one of the Welshman's famous breakfasts. Ball's only comment to his family was, 'It was very nice.'

On November 7th he reported to the RFC School of Aerial Gunnery at Hythe, where he was given elementary instruction in the workings of the Lewis and Vickers machine guns, and then retained briefly as an instructor. This unimaginative posting thoroughly depressed Ball, who expressed his feelings in no uncertain terms in a letter home:

> I am here and I know it. Of all the fools' games! Well, not only shall I pass away if I don't get a different job soon, but I really cannot think why they are such fools.

Even allowing for Ball's natural resentment at being 'reduced' to a run-of-the-mill weapons instructor, a task which could be, and usually was, done by any competent armament NCO, Ball had little interest in routine military duties. He had transferred to the RFC for one purpose only – to fight Germans in the air. The apparent absurdity of sending Ball, the RFC's leading fighter pilot, on a basic weapons course, and then employing him in a mundane ground instructional role, merely crystallized Ball's intention to return to France and the fighting zone. He therefore commenced a 'campaign' of dunning higher authority to permit him to return to the fighting. Ever solicitous of the possible effects of such a decision on his family, especially his mother, he wrote to her:

> I have offered to go out again and have another smack. I don't offer, dear, because I want to go,

but because every boy who has loving people and a good home should go out and stand up for it. You think I have done enough, but oh no, there is not, or at least should not be such a thought in such a war as this. Don't think me unfair wishing to go again, for I don't do it because I wish to. I shall find it hard to go, but you will all back me up, and I will try again to help my country and bring credit to my dear mother.

Ball's denial of a personal desire to rejoin the fighting was, perhaps, a permissible 'white lie', simply intended to soften the blow for his anxious mother. Like many other ex-operational pilots, Ball had found that he was at his most contented when with a front line squadron; only there was he fulfilled, where all life was reduced to a clear, uncomplicated dedication to his self-appointed vocation as a professional destroyer of his country's enemies.

His initial application was promptly refused, and he was coldly informed that his 'present work' was considered the best use to which his unique experience could be employed for the benefit of the Service. This bland rebuff merely angered Ball, who immediately ignored any future attempts to go through normal Service 'channels' and started to badger the highest authorities, using the strong influence of his father's friends in high places, or anyone else who had the ear of the War Office 'top brass'. He personally wrote to the Director of Air Organisation, Brigadier-General L E O Charlton, DSO, but Charlton, though expressing some sympathy with Ball's feelings, replied, in part, '... you will be sent out to France as soon as it is considered necessary that you should go, and there is no intention of keeping you in England a moment longer than the value of the work you are doing at present warrants.'

Unmollified, Ball stepped up his campaign. He next persuaded a Mr A Duckham of the Ministry of Munitions

– a friend of Ball's father – to speak on his behalf to General Sir David Henderson. Henderson, long in Army service and custom, was not prepared to entertain any such request when attempted by an 'old-boy' channel, and replied to Duckham somewhat stiffly, 'Captain Ball is at present employed in imparting his special knowledge to other officers, and that is the position in which I think he is, at present, most useful to the Service. He will get out to France again in good time, but he is not, himself, in a position to judge where his services are most useful.' This blunt reproof had no effect on Ball; he simply tried other means of achieving his goal.

In the meantime Ball was the recipient of several further honours and awards for his fighting prowess. On Saturday, November 18th 1916, Ball, his parents, sister Lois and brother Cyril, attended an investiture at Buckingham Palace, and from the hands of King George V, Ball received his DSO and two Bars* and a Military Cross. On the 24th of the same month the Nottingham City Council passed a resolution to make Albert Ball an Honorary Freeman of the City, a rare honour for one so young. On December 19th, in the Albert Hall, Nottingham, Ball was guest of honour at a large formal gathering of civic dignitaries, when he was presented with an illustrated address and a silver rose bowl, inscribed in tribute from the citizens of Lenton; the suburb of the city in which he had been born, and in which his father and grandfather had been born and raised.

In between these various ceremonies Ball's acknowledged expertise in flying fighter aircraft under operational conditions was put to some small use. On November 23rd he was detached for the day to the Royal Aircraft Factory at Farnborough, Hampshire, and whilst there had a brief test flight in the first prototype of an RAF-designed scout, the SE5 A4561. His opinion of the fighter is not recorded, but there seems little doubt that he

---

* The Second Bar to his DSO was gazetted on November 25th, 1916; thereby making Ball the first officer in the British Army to be awarded three DSOs.

Investiture. Ball outside Buckingham Palace on 18th November 1916 with (L-R): father, sister, Ball, a friend and his mother, having just been given his DSO and MC medals by HM King George V.

Presentation ceremony of a silver rose bowl to Ball from Lenton citizens, 19th December 1916

was not favourably impressed with its capabilities when he compared it privately with his favourite fighter, the Nieuport Scout. This 'bias' against the SE5 was soon to be expressed by Ball in blunt terms when, a little later, he was posted to the first unit to be fully equipped with SE5s, 56 Squadron RFC.

On January 2nd 1917, Ball reported to 7 Wing RFC at Kings Lynn, Norfolk for a further instructional post, but continued his efforts to obtain a posting back to France. He approached Lord Northcliffe, the press baron, who, typically, stormed the Whitehall bastions with his usual fervour. Whether Northcliffe's overtures were in any part responsible, or whether simple circumstance coincided is not known, but on February 17th 1917 Ball was officially notified that he was to join a new squadron being prepared

Ball, wearing his medals and displaying the casket containing his Freedom of Nottingham Scroll, February 1917

Posing for the press at Sedgley House, 19th February 1917

for operations in France; 56 (Training) Squadron, based at London Colney airfield in Hertfordshire.

Before moving to London Colney, however, Ball was given a short spell of leave to his home city Nottingham, where, on February 19th, with full pomp and ceremony, he was officially installed as an Honorary Freeman of the City. As such, Albert Ball was only the seventh Nottingham citizen to be so honoured since 1895 when the first was installed. His Freedom Scroll, a beautifully illuminated parchment, was presented in an ornate casket, silver on gilt, surmounted on its lid by a model Nieuport Scout.*

Presentation of Freedom of Nottingham to Ball on 19th February 1917 in the Exchange Hall. Front (L-R): Alderman E Huntsman, Albert's father, Sir J T McCraith, J Houston, E Mellor. 2nd row (L-R): Alderman F R Radford, Mayoress Mrs Pendleton, Albert Ball, Cllr J E Pendleton (Mayor), W J Board (Town Clerk), Deputy Town Clerk, Albert's mother

* Now (1977) in Nottingham Castle Museum.

Ball with his parents visiting his Trent College headmaster, J S Tucker, February 1917

Once the sumptuous celebrations were over, Ball returned to his unit, and arrived at London Colney in the evening of February 25th; being 'booked in' in the squadron officers' record book the following morning.

Elatedly he wrote home:

> Well, here I am and very nice too. General Henderson's son is here,* and many other good chaps. Tons of work is done and altogether it is a good place. My Flight is 'A' Flight, and I mean it to be 'A' in every way, also the men in it.

No 56 Squadron had officially come into being on June 8th 1916 at Gosport, and moved to London Colney in the following month, where it became an advanced training unit for pilots proceeding to France.

On February 6th 1917, Major R G Blomfield succeeded Major H D Harvey-Kelly as commanding officer of the squadron. An Australian-born ex-cavalry

---

* Captain Ian D H Henderson, who later joined 56 in France.

officer, and recently commander of 20 (Reserve) Squadron, Blomfield brought with him an excellent reputation as an organiser and administrator, and an equally high name as a disciplinarian of the best type. His personal terms of reference on appointment were to bring 56 Squadron from its present training role to fully operational status prior to moving to France. An additional responsibility was his knowledge that 56 had been selected to introduce the latest fighter design from Farnborough, the SE5.

Whilst awaiting delivery of its intended war equipment, 56 began receiving its pilots. Among the early arrivals were R T C Hoidge (January 15th), and a tall 19-years-old pilot already wearing the purple and white silk ribbon of a Military Cross, Cecil Lewis. These were soon joined by

Pilots of the newly-formed No 56 Squadron at London Colney airfield, April 1917. Standing (L-R): G C Maxwell, W B Melville, H M T Lehmann, C R W Knight, L Barlow, K J Knaggs. Seated (L-R): C Lewis, J O Leach, Major Blomfield (OC), Albert Ball, R T C Hoidge

Arthur Rhys-Davids, ex-captain of Eton; Gerald Maxwell, nephew of Lord Lovat and a veteran of the Gallipoli debacle; Leonard Barlow; J O Leach, MC, and others less experienced. All were to blossom into high-scoring fighting pilots in the months ahead, but were fortunate in having at London Colney such experienced men as Captains Cyril Crowe, A R Johnston and H V Dowling as instructors, who inculcated them into the 'arts' of aerial combat, and the new concepts of teamwork in the air.

With the average age of most of his pilots below 21, Major Blomfield took great care not to dampen their natural youthful enthusiasm for their main task. His sole concern was to create a first-class fighting unit, and towards that objective he had all pilots out for a strenuous run before breakfast each day; kept them busily occupied in the air or on hangar maintenance throughout the day, and then let them loose each evening to pursue their own pleasures. In particular, he ensured that the pilots had an absolute minimum of routine military duties and Service administrative drudgery. In this he was superbly aided by his Recording Officer the equivalent of today's squadron adjutant – Lieutenant T B Marson, a veteran of the Boer war and Gallipoli, who had lost his right leg in the latter campaign.

As a Flight commander, Albert Ball found he had plenty of work to occupy him, but he was now extremely happy; looking forward eagerly to his imminent return to the fighting zone in France. His personal contentment was enhanced on March 10th when an old friend and fighting companion, Captain Leslie Foot, joined 56 Squadron at London Colney.

Notification was received that the unit's allocation of operational aircraft were almost ready to be issued, and on March 13th Ball and Foot were sent to Farnborough to collect the first pair of SE5s. Both men left the factory on a private race to be the first to actually land in an SE5 at London Colney, but near Hendon Foot's SE was forced to land due to a broken oil pressure pipe, leaving Ball with the privilege of bringing in the squadron's initial example. Two days later another SE5, A4850, was delivered in crates to London Colney, where it was assembled and taken over by Ball as his personal aircraft. His reasons for selecting A4850 rather than a fully assembled aircraft soon became apparent. The initial SE5s sent to the squadron were fitted with a Vickers gun recessed into the upper fuselage in front of the cockpit; and an over-wing Lewis gun on a curved Foster-rail mounting. In place of the more usual small windscreen in front of the cockpit rim, a large celluloid, semi-enclosed windscreen was fitted, which part-enclosed the cockpit.

Ball, who had already formed a dislike for the design – based apparently solely on his brief acquaintance with the SE5 prototype the previous November – promptly set about 'refining' the aeroplane to accord with his personal requirements. He had the Triplex 'glass-house' discarded and replaced with a simple rectangular Avro wind-screen; the Vickers gun removed, and its location faired over in ply-wood; the external fuel tank above the centre-section of the top wing removed, and a new centre-section incorporating new water and fuel tanks internally fitted in its place. The standard undercarriage wheels of 700 x 100mm tyres were replaced by slimmer (700 x 75mm) equivalents. Inside the cockpit the production adjustable pilot's seat was exchanged for a wooden, fixed seat, and the tailplane controls modified accordingly. In the floor of the cockpit Ball had a second Lewis gun fitted to fire downwards at an angle, through a small clear-vision panel.

The result of all these refinements was a more streamlined forward fuselage contour, with the bonus of a few extra mph on the aircraft's speed. The value of the downward-firing Lewis gun was extremely doubtful, and it remains something of a mystery as to why Ball included this unorthodox armament. Removal of the Vickers gun, and its related synchronisation gun gear,

Three instructors for the embryo 56 Squadron. (L-R): Captains A R Johnston, H V Dowling, C M Crowe.
Cyril Crowe later joined 56 in France as a Flight Commander and was the last man to see Albert Ball alive
on Ball's ultimate sortie on 7th May 1917

permitted the installation of a slightly increased capacity main fuel tank in the fuselage, thereby offering extended endurance on any future patrols.

All these modifications had been completed before the end of March, and A4850 was finally assembled and ready for use. That Major Blomfield permitted Ball such a free hand in drastically modifying a brand-new aircraft to a purely personal standard was an indication of the high regard in which Ball was held by the squadron commander. A further, tiny example of this was provided by one of 56's ground crew, Corporal W Sadler, a photographer on the unit:

> I did not see Captain Ball for some days, but a mechanic told me one day where I could see him. I found him in dungarees – covered with oil – long black hair (which never seemed out of place) – working like any ordinary mechanic on his beloved machine. The next time I saw him he came along with Major Blomfield, the latter correctly dressed; Captain Ball with an oil-stained tunic, buff top boots covered with mud, no cap, and hands very deep in his breeches' pockets. Major Blomfield was a stickler for discipline. All officers and men were so correctly dressed as flying circumstances would permit – with one exception only, Captain Ball.*

It was in just such an unkempt state of dress that Ball first made the acquaintance of a young girl with whom he was to fall hopelessly and deeply in love, with all the fervour of an adolescent. Her name was Flora Young, an 18-years old vision of beauty. She was, at that time, resident in St Albans, and engaged in agricultural war work. A family friend, Mr Piper, with whom Albert Ball had once been billetted during his earlier Service days, had heard that Ball was in the area, and asked Flora to

* *The Boy Hero*, W A Briscoe.

"Bobs" – Flora Young with whom Ball became enraptured in March 1917

drive him to Shenley airfield where Ball and other pilots from 56 Squadron were engaged in some flying.

Flora had, of course, heard of Ball and his exploits, but had never met him personally. On arrival at Shenley she watched as two pilots walked over to her car to greet Mr Piper. One was J O Leach, but Flora took one look at the other – short, black-haired, unkempt in creased tunic and scruffy-looking flying-boots – and instinctively realised that this must be Albert Ball.

After the briefest of introductions, Ball turned to Flora and, in his usual direct manner, asked if she would like a 'flip' in an aeroplane. Flora said yes, and borrowing a leather flying coat from Leach, was promptly installed in an Avro 504 and taken aloft by Ball.

After the flight Ball stayed with Flora for a while, talking inconsequentially, but privately enraptured by this slim, beautiful girl in a pale lemon dress and yellow hat; her long hair in heavy rolled plaits 'put up' to frame her face. That night he wrote the first of many short letters to her, 'Just cannot sleep without first sending you a line to thank you for the topping day I have had with you. I am simply full of joy to have met you…'

The following day, March 26th, Ball saw Flora again, and wrote to her that evening:

> Dear Bobs – must call you Bobs for I don't like calling you 'Miss Young'. You don't mind do you? Well, I got back quite OK this morning but I am afraid they have all guessed. They always do…

'They' were the other pilots on 56 Squadron, who good-naturedly chaffed Ball about his new-found romance, but Ball was not offended – he was deeply, ardently happy. On the 27th Ball travelled to Farnborough, from where he flew another new SE5 to the squadron; the previous day one of the squadron pilots had crashed fatally, wrecking a new SE5 in the process.

On March 31st Major Blomfield received orders for his squadron to mobilize next day – it was about to be sent to France. Months of gradual preparation were crystallized into a week of furious activity and no little bustle, as a hundred and one last-minute details were attended to. Unofficial rumour of the imminent move had filtered through to the unit a few days before, and all pilots spent the last few days of March in packing their personal kit for onward transmission to France. Ball, in spite of his many Service duties then, contrived to spend every possible off-duty hour with Flora.

As a token of his feelings towards her, he gave her a small brooch of RFC 'wings', silver with diamond 'lights'. Typical of his bluntly direct approach in all things, he suddenly produced this gift as Flora was driving him back to the airfield one evening; the unexpectedness of the gift so surprised Flora she nearly ran the car into a ditch!

In the evening of Holy Thursday, April 5th, Ball as usual attended the local church service, in civilian clothes for anonymity, and then went to Flora's home for the rest of the evening. On Good Friday the pilots held a farewell dinner in a small hotel in nearby Radlett, but Ball slipped away early to be with Flora. That evening he virtually 'announced' to her that they were to be married after his spell in France, and in lieu of an engagement ring he gave her the small gold identity bracelet from his wrist.

Flora gave Ball a small compendium of Robert Louis Stevenson's prayers, and later in the dusk, at his request, sang for him his favourite tune, 'Thank God for a Garden'. Her lilting voice – she had once been trained for a possible operatic career – coupled with the knowledge that she had consented to his proposal, completed Ball's contentment.

Despite his entrancement with Flora, Ball could never forget his family, and in a final letter to them wrote:

I cannot leave dear old England without a word of thanks to you. It is hard to leave such dear people, but you are brave as well as dear and it makes it less hard. It is an honour to be able to fight and do one's best for such a country and for such dear people. I shall fight for you, and God always looks after me and makes me strong; may He look after you also.

It has been said in the past that Ball had some form of premonition before leaving England that he would never return. Whilst it is impossible to disprove this contention, there appears to have been very little evidence of such a foreboding beyond general remarks on the inevitably small odds for any fighting pilot to survive the war. His faith in his God was implicit, as indeed it had been from his earliest youth. His love for his family was unfailing. Now, he had the love of the girl he hoped to marry. Collectively, they provided Ball with every possibility of bright hope and a future in prospect.

Ball in SE5, A4850, London Colney, 7th April 1917. Behind, bare-headed, is Bill Young, brother of Flora Young

During his last leave in Nottingham he had, it is true, sorted and arranged all his private papers and possessions in neat, organised fashion, with instructions that nothing was to be disturbed until his return; but such a practical arrangement was merely in keeping with his usual tidiness of mind. Consistent with his strong sense of duty and honour, he entertained no thoughts of deferring or avoiding his posting to France; yet now, for perhaps the first time in his life, he had a goal in view – to return to Flora, and the promise of a future full of hope.

By April 5th the squadron had received its full complement of SE5s, and was almost ready to proceed to the war zone. On that date an advance party of ground crews with three officers, Lieutenant T B Marson, Second Lieutenant M A Kay, and an ex-60 Squadron veteran fighter pilot, the South African Captain H Meintjes, or 'Duke' as he was known to his friends, left for France by rail and boat. Meintjes had only joined 56 the day before.

By the morning of April 7th only the pilots and aircraft were left in England. Take-off was set for 11am, and Captain Leslie Foot had been originally detailed to lead the squadron, but on the evening of the 6th Foot was involved in a car accident and injured. The privilege of leading 56 to war was given to Cecil Lewis, who proudly tied a Flight commander's cloth streamers to his SE5s outer struts.

By 10am thirteen SE5s were lined along the edge of London Colney aerodrome, with Ball's A4850 slightly in front of the remaining dozen. Final farewells were made by each pilot to the many friends and relations who had come to see them go. Ball had refused to let Flora come to London Colney, so her father and brother came in her place.

Just before 11am Ball scribbled a brief note to Flora and handed it to her brother to give to her after his departure – it said simply, 'God bless you dear.'

OPPOSITE: *Last minute briefing of Ball in SE5, A4850, at London Colney, 7th April 1917*

56 Squadron about to leave London Colney for France at 1100hrs on 7th April 1917. Ball's SE5, A4850, seen in front

10

Back to France

A T precisely 11am on April 7th 1917, thirteen SE5s of
56 Squadron RFC, their Hispano-Suiza engines
revving in staccato deep-throated roars, began to edge
forward along the perimeter of London Colney
aerodrome, led by Cecil Lewis. Then, in quick succession,
their pilots sat high in the cockpits, they rolled forward
and got airborne. Last in the procession was A4850, its
pilot, Albert Ball, easily distinguishable by his lack of
flying helmet and goggles, his black hair dancing in the
howling slipstream.

Picking up a loose formation the SEs headed south
and, after refuelling in the southern counties, finally
headed out over the English Channel and eventually

Lt Cecil Lewis MC who led the squadron to France on 7th April 1917

landed intact at the RFC Depot at St Omer. Shortly
afterwards they were airborne again and within minutes
were landing at their designated war station, Vert Galand
aerodrome, situated 11 miles north of Amiens, alongside
the main Amiens-Doullens road. Here they came under
the aegis of 9th (Headquarters) Wing RFC; sharing the
airfield with 19 Squadron (Spad S7s) and 66 Squadron
(Sopwith Pups).

Within 48 hours the first battle of Arras was due to start,
and 9th Wing was responsible for air cover and co-
operation with the 4th and 5th British Armies, on the right
flank of the proposed offensive. The fighter squadrons from
Vert Galand were allotted a patrol area centred on Cambrai,
extending roughly to Le Cateau-Busigny-Solesmes-Denain.
However, due to the inexperience of most of its pilots, and
the fact that the SE5 was a completely new design in
France, 56 Squadron was forbidden to fly any war patrols
over the lines for its first two weeks in France.

Major Blomfield, wise in Service lore, had recognised
a need for drastically modifying his squadron's SE5s from
their factory-issue state to a more practical standard
before leaving England, but patiently waited until the unit
was in France – away from the immediate clutches of the
War Office bureaucrats – before instigating a crash
programme of aircraft modifications.

Primarily, he ordered the removal of all the issue-type
'greenhouse' windscreens, an obvious hazard to any pilot
both in combat and in everyday flying; having these
replaced by simple Avro windscreens of the type already
fitted on Ball's A4850. Other improvements were made to
the SE's armament, fuel tanks and undercarriages.
Blomfield then concentrated on training his pilots in the
rudiments of combat tactics, and generally familiarising
themselves with their 'war horses.'

His squadron establishment was completed on April
19th, when Captain Cyril Crowe joined the unit and took
command of B Flight.

Ball's first letter from France to Flora Young was written in the morning of April 10th, in which he complained:

We have not started work yet, and I don't think we shall do so for at least another week. All our kit is still in England, and will not be sent until about the 16th, so you can guess things are not very Cheer O!...

Later that day he jotted down a further note to her, in which he mentioned, 'In a few seconds I am going off with a pilot called Maxwell.* We are trying to make a hut in which we hope to sleep.' A letter to his father dated April 11th, however, touched on more serious matters:

They have put me on a SE5 machine but I should like to get back to my old machine as soon as possible; oh, I shall never be able to do my job. I must fly another machine and then I shall get along with the job.

Ball's initial dislike of the stationary-engined, and thus less manoeuvrable, SE5 when compared with his previous agile Nieuports had been a bone of contention with him since he first joined 56 Squadron; and previous letters home had expressed in blunt terms his anxiety at having to go to war – 'his job' – in what he considered an inferior aircraft design.

Ball's father had reacted typically by immediately badgering the highest RFC authorities to permit his son to have his wish, and be given a Nieuport. Correspondence between Ball's father and the GOC RFC, Hugh Trenchard reached a point where the gruff RFC commander became annoyed with the 'outside pressure'. His irritation did not interfere with his private opinion of young Ball, however.

---

* Later Wing Commander G C Maxwell MC, DFC, AFC, who died December 8th 1959.

On April 13th Ball wrote home, 'I had tea at the General's house today. He has decided to give me the machines I wanted.' To Flora that day he explained, 'Have just been to see the C-in-C and he has given me a Nieuport, also my SE, so all is now OK.'

On April 9th Ball had flown his SE5, A4850, to the RFC repair depot at Candas, and whilst there the machine underwent further modification. Ball's idea for a Lewis gun firing through the floor of his cockpit had already been frowned upon by higher authority, and on this date it was removed. A Vickers gun was replaced on the forward fuselage, fixed above the cowling in order that Ball could retain the slightly larger fuel tank already installed internally. In addition the original short exhaust pipes of the engine were exchanged for a pair of longer pipes, as on the Spad S7 scout. Finally a new, small Avro windscreen was fitted.

On the 13th Ball was again at Candas, from where he collected A4850, and was accompanied on the return flight to Vert Galand by 'Duke' Meintjes, who piloted the Nieuport 17 scout B1522, which had been allotted for Ball's personal use. Delighted to be back in the cockpit of his own Nieuport, Ball was up early the next morning, and took B1522 up for a 'practice flight' of nearly two hours. In the early evening, after several hours adjusting controls and armament (a single Lewis gun mounted above the upper wing on a Foster rail slide) to his own taste, Ball took the Nieuport up again for just over an hour. Officially both of these flights were listed in the squadron records as 'practice'; yet on the 14th Ball wrote to Flora:

> Oh! what a topping day it has been. First of all *I had my first two fights this morning.* In the first one the Hun ran off, but in the second I managed to get in a few rounds and made him run... (Italics are the author's.)

Ball then repeated his reference to these 'two fights' in his next letter to Flora, dated April 15th. No other record of these, apparently Ball's first encounters with German aircraft in 1917, have been traced; while his only *officially* recorded flight on April 14th was a 15-minute trip in his SE5 A4850 from Candas to Vert Galand. Yet it would have been entirely out of character for Albert Ball to have laid any sort of claim for something he had not in fact done, such was his essential honesty in all things.

Writing to Flora on the 18th, Ball said, 'Am feeling so very happy and OK. Today I have finished all my machines, moved all my Flight into one big hut, also have got my own but OK...' On the same day he told his family, 'All my machines and officers are at last ready for war. We hope to have a smack in a day or two... I have got another red cowl on my machine.'

This reference to a 'red cowl' is not entirely clear, in that he might have been referring to having the nose of his SE5 A4850 doped in the same colour – red – as his wheel discs; the A Flight marking. Equally, though less likely on available evidence, he could have been referring to a red spinner on his Nieuport B1522; or even a spinner on his SE5, though photographic evidence would seem to nullify this latter idea.

On April 21st Ball entered in his diary, 'Dud day, so flew to St Omer. Flew over lines at night (*sic*). Had scrap with two Albatros scouts, fired 12 drums, but only cleared them off'.

Again, there is no official record of any combats by Ball on this date among surviving documentation; though it is recorded that he left Vert Galand in his Nieuport at 11.25am, and eventually returned at 4pm. The reason for this absence is simply recorded as a 'test flight'. As with his 'fights' of April 14th, it can be only surmised that Ball, impatient to get to grips with the Germans again, and dutifully obeying the standing strict orders that no SEs might cross the lines yet, had simply seized the opportunity in his Nieuport to do a little 'free-lancing' without officially recording the outcome.

Finally, on April 22nd, 56 Squadron commenced operations. The honour of leading the unit's first war patrol fell to A Flight, and at 9.30am Ball led five other SE5s off from Vert Galand and headed towards the lines. The orders for this patrol were explicit; the six SEs were to patrol the line Lievin-Moreuil for two and a half hours 'this side of the lines', as high as possible, and were not to approach any nearer than two miles from the lines. A final note on the order read, 'On no account will an SE5 cross the lines under any circumstances.'

Ball, flying SE5 A4850, was accompanied by Knaggs (A4854), Maxwell (A4863), Barlow (A4858), Musters (A4860), and Kay (A4866). After 45 minutes of steady climbing, the SEs reached their patrol height of 11,000 feet and steadily flew above the area Aix-Nouville-St Leger. Almost at once Gerald Maxwell's aircraft engine

Lt Gerald Constable Maxwell of 56 Squadron, London Colney, 7th April 1917

developed trouble and he was forced to return to base, but the remaining SEs continued towards Lievin-Croiselles.

Ball's keen eyes soon spotted an Albatros two-seater, 1,000 feet higher, over Adinfer Wood. Firing a red Very light to indicate enemy aircraft, Ball immediately set off in pursuit. The German crew, *Leutnants* Richard Dietrich and Eckstein, had already seen their danger and Dietrich turned eastwards in a shallow dive. Ball managed to close to within 150 yards range, and fired three drums in quick succession from his upper-wing Lewis gun; but the Albatros escaped across the lines, apparently unscathed.

Mindful of his strict orders to stay on the British side of the lines, Ball gave up the chase, and led his men back to the patrol area; finally returning to Vert Galand just before 1pm. That afternoon another Flight made their first patrol, under the same restrictions, and failed to make any contact with German aircraft.

At 6am the following morning Ball took off alone in his Nieuport and patrolled expectantly over Cambrai. His patience was rewarded when he sighted two Albatros CIIIs above the town, and dived at them. Firing a short burst to confuse the gunners, Ball attempted to get underneath them for his accustomed bellyshot. The first Albatros immediately turned east and cleared, but Ball's fire ripped through the second machine, and the Albatros spun away to earth. Following it down, Ball continued firing and the two-seater crashed alongside the Tilloy-Abancourt road. Neither of its crew got out of the wreckage.

Climbing to 5,000 feet Ball next noticed another two-seater Albatros south-east of Arras, in the clouds. In his haste to attack Ball dived and overshot the German machine, and its gunner promptly put a burst through the Nieuport's wings, piercing both spars with 15 bullets before his pilot escaped into cloud again. Ball nursed his damaged machine back to Vert Galand and landed safely, though the Nieuport was thereby out of commission for several days while repairs were effected.

Two hours later Ball was again airborne, alone, flying
SE5 A4850, and patrolling between Arras and Cambrai.
Sighting an Albatros two-seater going south over Adinfer
at 12,000 feet, Ball came up under its tail and, at 100
yards, fired his Lewis gun – only to have the gun jam after
five rounds. The Albatros put down its nose and fled,
whilst Ball went down to land at Filescamp airfield, home
of his former unit 60 Squadron.

Having rectified his Lewis, Ball took off again,
climbing towards Cambrai.

Just before noon he spotted a tight formation of five
Albatros scouts over the town, all doped mainly in a pale
green finish. Odds meant little to Ball who immediately
chased the Germans, closing with them over Selvigny.
Selecting the nearest Albatros, Ball poured 150 rounds of
one-in-three tracers into its slender fuselage at close range.
The German staggered and dropped away, then burst into
flames; the burning remnants fluttering to earth.*

Outpacing its four companions, Ball climbed hard and
soon found himself approaching an all-white Albatros
two-seater at 12,000 feet on the north side of Cambrai. At
100 yards he fired the remaining ammunition in his Lewis
gun, and watched it fall away erratically to eventually
make an apparently safe landing. Unbeknown to Ball his
bullets had found their mark. The Albatros CIII was from
Flieger-Abteilung 7, based at Awoingt, and its observer,
Leutnant Berger, had received a severe neck wound,
leaving the German pilot, *Vizefeldwebel* Ebert, little
choice but to reach safety as quick as possible. Berger
died in hospital eventually on May 15th 1917.

Writing to Flora that evening Ball summarised his
successes:

Have got my first two Huns down today. I had
three fights and managed to bring one down crashed

---

* Hitherto identified as *Hauptmann* Paul Hennig Adalbert Theodor von Osterroht, leader of
Jagdstaffel 12. However, von Osterroht was killed on an *evening* patrol on this date.

in a road. This I did with my Nieuport. After coming down I had to have new planes, for the Hun had got about 15 shots through my spars. Well, next I went up in my SE5 and had a poo-poo time. Five shots in my right strut, four in the planes, and two just behind my head. This was done by five Albatros scouts, but I got one of them and set it on fire at 14,000 feet. Poor old chap inside. I should simply hate to be set on fire. The General (*Trenchard... Author*) rang me up and congratulated me, also the CO of our Wing. I am keeping the strut and shall give it to you when I come home.

In a brief note to his parents Ball admitted that the day's high tension and activities had exhausted him – 'Am so fagged tonight...' These combats – the first of 56 Squadron's eventual prodigious 'scoreboard' of victories – were curious in one respect. Despite his SE5s two-gun armament, Ball made no use of his fuselage Vickers gun; relying instead on the wing-mounted Lewis gun, the well-tried technique he had always used in his Nieuports of 1916.

On April 24th Ball flew two fighting patrols in SE5 A4850, but despite contacts with German aircraft, had to suffer the frustration of having his guns jam several times. The new SE5s, with their temperamental engines, and Vickers guns synchronised by the new Constantinesco gun-gear, were not yet thoroughly familiar to either air crews or ground crews; and many possible successes in these first few weeks of 56's fighting career ended without result due to various purely mechanical failures in the machines. Nevertheless, individual pilots managed to emulate Ball's opening victories, as Ball explained to Flora that evening:

Have just come in from a patrol. I had one fight with an Albatros but the dear old thing ran away so I did not get a good chance. The squadron now has five Huns. One was got by Lieutenant Barlow of B Flight.* The other four have been got by my Flight, A. Lieutenant Maxwell got one this morning, and Lieutenant Knaggs this afternoon, and I got the other two yesterday. Not bad is it? I am so pleased my Flight is top.

The following day was a 'dud' one, bad weather conditions preventing any worthwhile air operations, and Ball took the opportunity to improve his private accommodation, and, as during his days with 11 and 60 Squadrons the previous year, started planting out a small vegetable and flower garden. Not content with simply making his hut more comfortable, he commenced construction of an adjoining greenhouse, and gathered the necessary plumbing equipment for a proposed hot water system, including a bath and overhead shower fitting. As always, it was not in Ball's nature to be idle, even when the opportunity for a restful, lazy day occurred; he constantly needed activity in order to be happy.

Ball's diary entry for April 26th was brief, 'Dud day. Went on patrol, saw nothing. At night, cleared up, so went up and attacked 20 Huns. I got two of them at Cambrai. Arrived back at dark with all ammunition used up.'

That evening Ball had set out in A4850 to patrol the Lens-Arras area, taking off at 6.15pm. An hour later, flying at 13,000 feet, he noticed a loose formation of FE2bs coming from the direction of Cambrai, but then spotted a number of German scouts leaving their airfield east of the town, presumably intent on attacking the FEs. Ball bided his time, letting the enemy scouts come up to him.

When these reached about 6,000 feet, Ball dived, his Lewis gun and Vickers both firing to within 60 feet of the first Albatros. The scout fell sideways and tumbled crazily

---

* Lieutenant Leonard M Barlow, who eventually scored 18 victories; was awarded a Military Cross and two Bars, but died on February 5th 1918, at Martlesham Heath in England, when the wings of the Sopwith Dolphin (C3779) he was testing collapsed in the air and crashed, burning.

into a wood north-east of Cambrai. Ball turned for the lines but found his way blocked by the remaining five Albatri. Tackling these head-on, his Vickers gun blazing, Ball attempted to break through but failed, and therefore flew south-eastwards. The Albatri followed, with one DIII painted light brown outpacing his companions. As this scout came within firing range, Ball turned swiftly, dived, and fired the rest of his Vickers and Lewis ammunition into it until he almost collided. The Albatros erupted in flames along the right side of its fuselage and dropped out of sight, leaving a pall of smoke to mark its downward path.

Almost immediately the remaining Germans were upon Ball, lacing his SE5 with bullets. Using his remaining two spare drums of Lewis ammunition, Ball fired these at a long-tailed, shark-nosed scout, which spun down, apparently under control. Continuing south, Ball was now completely out of ammunition, but in the gathering dusk he finally managed to lose his attackers, and soon was able to cross the lines and return to Vert Galand, landing just after 8.30pm.

Damage to SE5 A4850, was again widespread; that night the ground crew had to fit a new upper centre-section, a new starboard lower wing; patch an aileron, and patch over several bullet holes in the fuselage. By dawn it was ready again for Ball, who spent the day air-testing both the SE5 and his Nieuport, but flying no patrols until the mid-afternoon, when he took off in his Nieuport alone. Finding no opponents he returned to base, and after tea set out again in the SE, with the same result.

In his daily letter to Flora that evening he wrote,

> I have now got another two Huns, making four this time, and my total is now 34. Only three more to get before I am top of England and France again. In order to whack the German man (Boelcke) I have got about ten more to get. If it is God's will that I should do it then I will come home.

Ball went on to say that his personal hut was now finished, and that he now had '... a topping little greenhouse.' At 4pm on the 28th Ball, in A4850, led three of his Flight – Knight, Knaggs and Maxwell – on an offensive patrol over the area Lens-Le Forest-Fontaine-Moreuil. At 8,000 feet above the Cambrai-Bapaume road Ball sighted three Albatros two-seaters below, over Cambrai, fired a red Very light to alert his companions, and led them in a dive on the German trio.

Firing his Vickers only to within 150 yards of one Albatros, Ball was frustrated by yet another gun jam, and banked away to correct the stoppage. His intended victim dived away to safety. All four SEs climbed and dived for a second attack on the remaining pair of Germans; one of which planed earthwards to land near Noyelles, though apparently under control. Climbing again, the SEs now dived on the remaining two-seater, and Ball closed to pointblank range, firing his Vickers in a continuous burst. The Albatros, shot to pieces, fell and was completely wrecked at Fontaine, west of Cambrai.

By this time the SE formation had broken up. Gerald Maxwell, in A4863, reached 12,000 feet but was almost immediately the target for some particularly accurate anti-aircraft fire, which hit his engine and shattered his elevator controls. With no power and only minimal control, Maxwell managed to turn his SEs headlong plunge to earth into a flattish glide towards the British trenches nearly ten miles away. Eventually, at a ground speed of about 140mph, Maxwell's SE5 hit the ground at Station 126, Deauville railway, near Combles. On contact the whole front part of the SE, including its engine, broke off; and the hapless Maxwell was bounced across the shell-broken surface in the remaining section of the fuselage for almost 100 yards before coming to a final stop. Gingerly inspecting himself for injuries, Maxwell could hardly believe his luck when he found that he was totally unscathed.

Meanwhile Ball, unable to find his men, climbed above cloud to continue his patrol, and soon came upon an Albatros two-seater over Epehy. At once he gave chase until he closed to 50 yards, when he commenced firing from both guns. The Albatros dived and eventually levelled out only 500 feet above the ground, with Ball still following and firing.

Intent only on his target, Ball failed to notice his dangerously low height, and was almost at once the focal point for an intense barrage of groundfire. The bursting shrapnel shredded Ball's SE5, cutting virtually all rudder and aileron controls, leaving him with merely his left elevator, controlled by just one top wire, with which to manoeuvre. Awoken to his peril, Ball eased the SE out of the firing and delicately nursed it towards the British lines.

Back at Vert Galand the other squadron pilots were anxiously looking eastwards for any sign of the 'missing' Maxwell and Ball, when they saw Ball's SE5 approaching very low. Cecil Lewis described the scene thus:*

> We saw him coming in rather clumsily to land. He was not a stunt pilot, but flew very safely and accurately, so that, watching him, we could not understand his awkward floating landing. But when he taxied up to the sheds we saw his elevators were flapping loose – controls had been completely shot away! He had flown back from the lines and made his landing entirely by winding his adjustable tail plane up and down! It was incredible he had not crashed. His oil tank had been riddled, and his face and the whole nose of the machine were running with black oil.

In his letter to Flora next day Ball only commented briefly on the whole episode, but went on to say, 'General

* *Sagittarius Rising* by C Lewis; Peter Davies, 1936.

Trenchard came to see me today and congratulated me. He asked me if I would like two weeks in England, but dear I think I had better stay until all is OK and the month up.'

His reference to 'the month up' concerned a verbal undertaking authorised by Trenchard that Ball would only stay in France for the first month of 56 Squadron's operations, in order to provide some veteran example to the many inexperienced pilots of the unit. There appears to be little doubt that Trenchard only agreed originally to Ball going to France to avoid any further nuisance on the part of Ball's father, friends and acquaintances who had 'campaigned' so vociferously on Ball's behalf. Yet Trenchard, a shrewd judge of character, had seen too many youngsters with the 'do-or-die' attitude of Ball who had been needlessly killed in action long after they might have been honourably withdrawn from the fighting. With good fortune, he hoped to spare Ball from over-extending himself; hence the imposed time limit on Ball's tour of action.

The damage to Ball's SE5 A4850, in the combats of the 28th was considerable, and that evening the machine was dismantled and sent to the Candas repair depot for major repairs. These included two new longerons, new fuselage cross-members, three-ply behind the seat; a new starboard wheel, completely new control wiring, and a full set of interplane struts. Once repaired, much of the bullet-riven fabric outer covering was replenished.

As a temporary replacement Ball flew SE A4858 for the evening patrol of April 29th, but as he led his men down onto a German aircraft over Adinfer, first his Lewis

PAGES 177-179: *Four views of Albert Ball in his personally modified SE5, A4850 at London Colney. He was killed in this aircraft on 7th May 1917*

and then his Vickers gun jammed hopelessly. Disgusted, Ball fired two green Very lights to indicate he was going back, and returned to his airfield.

On the last day of April he did little flying beyond a brief flight in his Nieuport B1522; but early that morning 56 Squadron suffered its first operational casualty when Second Lieutenant M A Kay, in SE5, A4866 was shot down and killed behind the German lines. In the afternoon of May 1st Ball travelled to nearby Candas to check progress on the refurbishing of his A4850, but specifically to ferry back to the squadron a new SE5, A8898.

That evening he was at the controls of A8898 when he set out with C R W Knight and H M T Lehmann for a patrol over the area Arras-St Hilaire-Bautouzille. Over

Ball, in SE5, A8907, at the Candas RFC Depot, France on 3rd May 1917

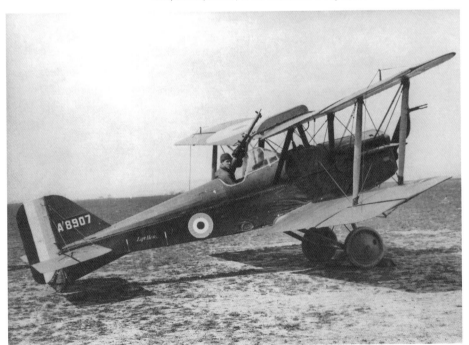

Cambrai a batch of six Albatros two-seaters was sighted. Climbing swiftly for advantageous height, Ball then led the SEs down in a plunging assault. Taking the leader as his prey Ball got in a burst of Vickers around its tail, before he was in turn attacked from behind. Turning quickly, Ball slid down his Lewis gun and fired a brief burst. The Albatros dived but Ball chased after it and fired a further 50 rounds from his Vickers. The German never came out of his dive, crashing alongside a road near Marquion.

Picking up his two companions south-west of Cambrai, Ball continued patrolling for nearly an hour before seeing a number of Albatros two-seaters coming in his direction near Cambrai. At two miles from the lines the two formations clashed; Ball firing his Lewis at an all-black machine which quickly left the combat eastwards. Just below him Ball saw a white Albatros and dived, firing his Vickers, but soon lost sight of his opponent as it seemed to go to ground near some trenches south-west of Cambrai.

Though Ball had maintained his customary intensive routine of flying whenever possible from dawn to dusk each day, an accumulation of factors was beginning to tell on him already. The fractiousness of his guns – a fault he shared with many other pilots in the squadron – was one source of frustration and continual anti-climax. Having to fly unfamiliar aircraft added to his general discomfort. Most important however was the increase in sheer pace of the air war generally, when compared with the heyday of his fighting career in the previous summer. On his return to France Ball had made no adjustment to the significant changes in air tactics and fighting incumbent by April 1917. One might truthfully say that he had simply 'picked up the reins' at precisely the point that he had laid them down the previous October. Yet the opposing air service had changed considerably in content and policy during Ball's absence in England.

By April 1917 the RFC was opposed by well-equipped *Jagdstaffeln*, containing many pilots with lengthy experience in air fighting. Witness to the Germans' prowess was the fact that in this month, 'Bloody April' as it came to be called, the RFC experienced its worst month of the war in the context of the proportion of air crews missing, killed or seriously wounded in action. Added to this, the experimental policy on the German side of temporarily banding several fighting *Staffeln* together for short-term tactical advantage was beginning to prove successful.

On April 30th, directly opposing the 9th Wing RFC units, which included 56 Squadron, four *Jagdstaffeln*, Nos 3, 4, 11 and 33, were so grouped. In their ranks were many of the contemporary leading 'aces', including *Rittmeister* Manfred von Richthofen, leader of *Jagdstaffeln* 11 and, by that date, credited with more than 50 victories. The war skies were now seldom empty; enemy met enemy on almost every flight; combats were now more frequent, and more deadly.

If Albert Ball recognised in himself the now familiar signs of combat exhaustion, he gave no outward clue to its existence. If he had become aware of the much stiffer opposition that he was by now meeting, he made no comment but simply continued to fight in the only way he knew or understood, by constant flying, and by attacking everything and anything which opposed him, utterly regardless of mathematical odds against him. His fundamental innocence of guile or cunning remained evident until the day he died. His fighting creed was totally uncomplicated; his pursuance of his personal ideal of duty was all-embracing.

11

Fights and Foes

THE frustrating gun-jamming continued to nullify Ball's efforts on May 2nd, when, flying SE5 A8898, he led C R W Knight and H M T Lehmann on a fighting sortie over the Cambrai-Arras-Douai sector, hunting for German airmen. From 12,000 feet he dived on a brown-green camouflaged Albatros two-seater west of Cambrai, and fired a few rounds of Vickers at 150 yards range, only to see the German put its nose down and escape further attack. Minutes later, he spotted another two-seater further south and dived until he was within a few yards, only to have his Vickers gun jam.

Leaving the German, Ball landed at 60 Squadron's airfield, had the gun rectified, and took off again immediately in the direction of Arras. Near the lines east of this town he sighted two more Albatros two-seaters and promptly dived to attack. Again his Vickers gun jammed, and the Albatri cleared the area. With only his Lewis gun operative, Ball then joined in a combat over Douai where three Nieuports were hard-pressed with a crowd of Albatros. This time the Lewis refused to function smoothly, and Ball was forced to abandon the patrol and return to Vert Galand.

That evening, flying SE A4855, in company with K J Knaggs (A4854), Ball prowled the air above Bailleul-Courchelettes-Tilly-Ecoust at 13,000 feet. About 7.30pm he noticed four red-painted Albatros DIIIs between Douai and the trenches, going south. Diving at the nearest, Ball nearly ran into a trap. No sooner had he plunged onto his intended victim than another four or five Albatri piled down onto his tail. Ball banked steeply, pulled down his Lewis gun, and waited for his attackers to close.

Captain E L Foot, Ball's close friend in Nos 11, 60 and 56(R) Squadrons, seated in an SE5

The first Albatros fired at Ball but overshot him, to which Ball replied with a crisp burst from his Vickers. As the impetus of the Albatros' dive took it flashing past Ball's SE, Ball whipped behind its tail and, with the tenacity of a terrier, clung to this position all the way down to 2,000 feet; all the time riddling the German with his Vickers gun. The red Albatros, with engine at full power, bored straight into some rough ground between Halte and Vitry.

Climbing again, Ball found that the general dogfight above him now included about a dozen RFC aircraft – some Sopwith Pups, Bristol F2as and FE2bs – milling round in a motley scrimmage with some 20 German fighters. Circling and manoeuvring for a favourable position, Ball fastened on the tail of a white German scout with a very pointed nose and hammered in a lengthy burst of Vickers. The German flicked over into a steep dive and cleared, apparently unhurt. By then the general combat was drifting towards Douai, with the Germans being out-manoeuvred and yielding air to their British opponents.

Ball left them and flew southwards to Cambrai, from where he spotted a lone white two-seater Albatros over Sailly. Diving almost vertically on this machine, he put some good bursts of Vickers and a full drum of Lewis into it from 100 to 25 yards range. The Albatros literally dropped from the sky, but the gathering dusk – it was now 8.10pm – prevented Ball from observing its fate. The German crew, *Vizefeldwebel* Seifert (pilot) and *Unteroffizier* Niess, from Flieger-Abteilung 26, were both mortally wounded. Their Albatros fell behind British lines near Vitry-en-Artois, and both men were made prisoner, but died later.

Ball spent the following day, May 3rd, at Candas repair depot, flying his SE5 A8898 over, and air-testing his Nieuport B1522 whilst there. He eventually flew A8898 back to Vert Galand in mid-evening. Whilst at Candas he wrote a long (for him) letter to Flora, his first in several days. 'Am so very sorry dear that I have been so long in writing again, but I have been having such a poo-poo time.' He then summarised his exploits of the previous three days, particularly the many frustrating gun jams, and then continued:

> You don't know what a beastly game it is, when nothing is going as it should, and you have not got

"The Frenchman" mentioned by Ball in a letter home. The ace, Capitaine Georges Guynemer

enough men to do the jobs. Last night I came in off patrol, got two Huns, and was feeling very pleased with life. The squadron gave a concert at night and I went. Everyone was very pleased for I am now one in front of the Frenchman [*Georges Guynemer*]. My total is 38.

All went well until about 10pm when the fire bell went. I rushed out and Oh! try to picture how pleased I was when I saw my hut, greenhouse and bathroom on fire. Well, I nearly had a double fit. I had taken so much trouble getting it nice, so that when I came in at night I could have a few hours real rest. The fire was caused by Lieutenant Knaggs leaving a candle on a box in his room. I have to laugh although I am really very cross... Am just longing to be with you again, and when I have made my total 40 I will come. I have only two more to get. The General (Trenchard) is giving me two SE5s, so I shall be OK.

This last remark is the first indication that Ball had now reconciled himself to the SE5 as his fighting machine. Though he retained his Nieuport, he had by now come to appreciate the ruggedness of the SE5 and its ability to absorb considerable battle damage; whilst the two guns offered him far greater firepower in actual combat. Less manoeuvrable than the Nieuport, nevertheless the SE's stability and heavier engine gave Ball a steadier gun platform, and a faster dive, this last virtue being of particular value in his contemporary fighting style of diving attacks.

More gun troubles robbed Ball and his companions of possible victims in the early hours of May 4th. Taking off in A8898 at a little after 5am, Ball was accompanied by two men from his Flight, Gerald Maxwell and K J Knaggs (in SEs A4854 and A8902); their objective being an offensive patrol (OP) over Cambrai-Douai-Lens-Vitry, seeking German aircraft. Searching first over Cambrai they found no opposition, so Ball headed north to Douai-Lens and at 6am spotted an Albatros two-seater some 5,000 feet below. All three SEs dived to attack, but the German crew were alert and promptly fled low down eastwards towards Douai. Closing to within 300 yards the SEs commenced long-range firing, but immediately suffered gun jams. The Albatros was lost to view, so the SEs started to climb back to 12,000 feet to continue their hunt.

Between Lens and Douai Ball spotted eight German scouts* about 2,000 feet higher. On trying to reach these, however, they saw the formation climb higher and make off eastwards. The SE pilots next spotted a pair of Albatros two-seaters at about 8,000 feet over Vitry, and

* Ball described these as 'Nieuport-type': possibly referring to Siemens DI, virtually a carbon copy of the Nieuport 16 Scout in design.

Ball led them down in a headlong dive. Reaching a range of only 200 yards the SEs again suffered gun jams after only a few rounds had been fired, and the German duo made off east, their gunners continuing to fire until well out of reasonable range. Levelling out at 6,000 feet the three SE pilots sighted yet another four Germans above them, but as they climbed to engage the Germans made off east climbing hard. Low on fuel, three thoroughly frustrated SE pilots returned to Vert Galand at 7.30pm, cursing their obstreperous guns.

After lunch Ball flew his Nieuport to Candas briefly and soon returned; and at 5.30pm took off with Maxwell and Knaggs to have another hunt for Germans; this time in the Vitry-Lens-Halte-Beaumont area. Striking north-west, they climbed to 11,000 feet and crossed the lines, and immediately saw eight Albatros scouts near Riencourt at their own level. Climbing slightly first, the SEs got above the Albatri, then dived, each man selecting his target. Ball tackled the nearest Albatros to him, putting in brief bursts from his Vickers which caused the German pilot to leave his formation and make towards Douai.

Switching to another Albatros, Ball bore in close and the German commenced a dive. Hanging grimly onto its tail, Ball fired a long burst of Vickers, and then dropped below its tail at almost touching range, from which position he slammed half a drum of Buckingham tracers into its plywood fuselage. The Albatros dropped away and crashed near Graincourt – its fate being later confirmed by a British anti-aircraft gun crew.

The remaining Albatri now scattered in all directions and the SEs, two suffering from jammed guns, went down to cross the lines and land at Baizieux, home of 23 Squadron, to replenish fuel and ammunition, and to tend to the recalcitrant guns. As they were about to take off again, Maxwell's SE, A4854, refused to start, so Ball and Knaggs left him and climbed as fast as possible towards Douai.

As they sped above the Arras road, Ball noticed two

Albatros two-seaters flying low below him near Vitry and began his dive to tackle them. Halfway down the SEs were met by four red-painted Albatros DIIIs, and Ball and Knaggs quickly took up the challenge of this latest opposition. After a series of circling manoeuvres, both SEs managed to get on the tails of opponents and Ball managed to sink a burst of Vickers into his target before the Albatri cleared downward and away from the fight.

Ball hardly had time to catch his breath before he was jumped by a large gaggle of Albatros scouts and two-seaters. Over Beaumont Ball twisted and turned, firing crisp bursts from each gun as targets presented themselves fleetingly. On at least two occasions he contrived to get on the tails of his antagonists, and in each case his accurate fire caused the Germans to dive away steeply to earth, though seemingly under control. Still manoeuvring, Ball lined his sight on a third Albatros, only to have both guns jam. Turning towards the lines, Ball easily outdistanced his pursuers due to the superior speed of his machine.

On May 5th, whilst the squadron armourers gave a full overhaul to the guns and synchronising gear on SE5 A8898, Ball reverted to his Nieuport, B1522, for a morning patrol. In company with Gerald Maxwell, he searched for enemy aircraft above Hesdin and the adjacent locality, but after an hour's fruitless flying, he returned to base. By mid-afternoon A8898 was declared serviceable and Ball took it up for a brief air test before tea.

Then, at 6pm, he led five of his Flight, flying A8898, out on a fighting patrol of the skies over the Douai-Cambrai sector. Within minutes two SEs dropped away, suffering engine troubles, and returned to the airfield. Ball carried on, with Cecil Lewis, Reginald Hoidge and W B Melville, but on nearing Douai these three climbed into cloud, and Ball was left alone.

Flying towards Lens, Ball broke into a clear sky, crossed the lines, and travelled north-east at 8,000 feet. One thousand feet higher he noticed two Albatros DIII

scouts approaching from the direction of Douai; their
white wings contrasting with pale brown fuselages. Ball
commenced climbing for height in the direction of
Carvin; the pair of Albatri still tracking him. On reaching
11,000 feet Ball found one DIII behind him and only
about 200 yards away.

Kicking his rudder hard, Ball reversed his flight path
and came up under the Albatros; then slid back his Lewis
gun and poured two full drums into the German in rapid
succession. The Albatros never wavered, flying steadily
on, but as Ball fired his third drum, its pilot came to life
and tried to escape. Ball followed on its tail, fired both
guns at deadly short range, and the Albatros fell to earth.

As the Albatros fell away, its companion arrived on the
scene and Ball climbed quickly, attempting to fasten on its
tail. His chance never came for the second Albatros turned
and, with both of its guns firing, attacked Ball head-on.
Ball did not evade his charge, but pressed his Vickers gun
trip and kept it pressed, firing one-in-one Buckingham
tracers at the approaching Albatros.

The Albatros continued to come at him, nose-on, its
guns still firing, and Ball afterwards admitted that he
thought the German meant to ram him. Nevertheless,
Ball refused to veer away as the German scout loomed
large in his windscreen.

The next few seconds were almost a blank to Ball. His
SE5 took a bullet in its oil tank and Ball's windscreen,
head and shoulders were blacked out with the viscous
fluid, blinding Ball temporarily. At that moment Ball
resigned himself to death. As the oil cut out his vision, he
instinctively hauled back on his control column,
frantically wiping the sticky fluid from his eyes. His
vision cleared, and on looking around he could find no
sign of his opponent in the air. With no oil pressure and an
engine liable to overheat and seize at any moment, Ball
put the SE into a gentle dive to 3,000 feet; from which
height he found his two victims, both wrecked on the

ground, and within 400 yards of each other.

Making towards the lines, his nerves completely exhausted by his brush with almost certain death, Ball encountered two more German aircraft near Lens, but avoided these and finally scraped home to Vert Galand, his SE5 bearing grim witness to the recent fighting. The squadron Recording Officer, T B Marson, described Ball's immediate reactions to this fight:

> Flushed in face, his eyes brilliant, his hair blown and dishevelled, he came to the squadron office to make his report, but for a long time was in so over-wrought a state that dictation was an impossibility to him. 'God is very good to me.' 'God must have me in His keeping.' 'I was certain he meant to ram me.' The possibility that his opponent, finding himself mortally hit, had determined to have a life for a life occurred to him. In that event his nerve failed him at the last.*

Just before midnight that evening Ball confided, in a letter to his father:

> One tried to ram me after he was hit and only missed by inches. Am indeed looked after by God, but Oh! I do get tired of always living to kill, and am really beginning to feel like a murderer. Shall be so pleased when I have finished.

To Flora Young he wrote:

> Well, I made my total 40 last night, and General Trenchard rang up to say I am going to be presented to General Sir Douglas Haig tomorrow. Oh, won't it be nice when all this beastly killing is over, and we can just enjoy ourselves and not hurt anyone.

* *Scarlet and Khaki*, T B Marson.

Describing to her the details of his latest successes, Ball concluded his letter:

This makes my 42nd, and the major is pleased. Re-hut and garden. Well, I have got it nearly right again now; in fact, I have just been lighting the petrol stove in my bath tank so that I may have a bath.

By the morning of May 6th, Ball's nervous system would appear to have fully recovered from its ordeal of the previous evening. Spending the best part of the morning in tending his little garden, Ball then drove to Candas where he collected his now fully serviceable SE5 A4850 and flew it back to the squadron. The remainder of the afternoon was taken up with attending to his guns and engine; checking, harmonising the guns to his personal requirements, and generally satisfying himself that the SE was in perfect order.

Ball with Captain Cyril M Crowe MC, DFC

That evening he flew his Nieuport B1522 on the 7pm patrol. Leading four SE5s, piloted by Captain Cyril Crowe, Lieutenants Cecil Lewis, Leonard Barlow and K J Knaggs, towards the Arras-Douai-Cambrai area, Ball's slower Nieuport was soon lagging behind the SEs and eventually lost touch with them near Arras. It mattered little to Ball, who preferred a lone hand, and had never been very comfortable fighting in the company of others.

Carrying on towards Douai, he soon sighted four red-coloured Albatros DIIIs a thousand feet below, heading in the direction of Cambrai. Ball lifted one wing and dived directly at the centre of this formation; firing a crisp burst of Lewis to confuse them as he came into range. As the Albatri formation broke wildly, Ball fastened under the fuselage of *Vizefeldwebel* Jäger's Albatros and riddled it with two and a half drums of one-in-one Buckingham tracers. The red Albatros faltered, paused, and then spun down to crash south of Sancourt village. Evading the other three Albatri, Ball flew back to Vert Galand, landing there a little after 8.30pm.

That evening Ball was content. He had accomplished all that he had set out to do; bringing his personal tally of 'victories' to an acknowledged top position among contemporary Allied fighting pilots. His promised 'month only' in France was technically 'up' on the following day, and therefore he could reasonably expect to be sent back to England within a few days; back to his beloved family, and to Flora, the girl he hoped to marry. Unbeknown to Ball, on this same day, May 6th, his Wing Commander, Lieutenant-Colonel Cyril N Newall, had written a letter to the OC 56 Squadron, Major Blomfield:

> Will you please send me a full report on what Ball has done since he came out with you. The report to including following:
> a) His statements (ie Combat Reports).
> b) What any other pilots have seen him do.

c) Condition of his machine after returning to the aerodrome on various occasions.

d) Any other points you may think of, and any confirmation of machines destroyed.

I would like this as soon as possible.

Blomfield received this letter the following morning, and replied on May 8th, enclosing Ball's combat reports with a covering letter. The purpose and intent of Newall's request, including the note of urgency for compliance, leaves little doubt that Ball was about to be recommended for the award of a Victoria Cross prior to his imminent posting to England. No other award would have been tenable; he already wore all the other possible decorations which might have been bestowed upon him.

However, deep and careful research over a long period has failed to unearth any substantiating evidence to fully support this contention; it must therefore remain a minor 'mystery' as to precisely the reasons behind Newall's request. Certainly, such a recommendation, at that period of the war, would not have been untoward. Albert Ball had achieved a fighting record second to none in the whole of the British flying services' history to date; whilst his personal example had become an inspiration to the whole of the Allied air services. It would not be invidious to suggest that, by that date, no member of the Royal Flying Corps was more worthy of the supreme honour.

12

May 7th 1917

MONDAY, May 7th 1917 started as just another working day for 56 Squadron. The weather was clear, with a bright spring sunshine, though the forecast threatened cloud and rain later. Just after mid-day the squadron was due for an escort patrol, protecting nine Sopwith 1½ Strutters of 70 Squadron from Fienvillers, on a photographic reconnaissance mission of certain German airfields.

Albert Ball spent his morning in checking over his SE5 A4850, and tending his thriving garden plot. At 12.30pm, in his SE5, he took off from Vert Galand in company with K J Knaggs (SE5, A8904) and Gerald Maxwell (A8902), climbing quickly to the pre-arranged rendezvous with the Sopwith two-seaters at 9,000 feet.

Once assembled the formation set course for the lines; the three SEs above and slightly ahead of their charges. The objectives for 70 Squadron's cameras were the German flying grounds at Caudry and Neuvilly, and the outward journey met no air opposition apart from some isolated and inaccurate anti-aircraft bursts of fire. Over their targets the Sopwith crews plodded patiently back and forth over the German bases exposing all plates and then, their mission completed, turned for home. Over Beauvois a solitary German two-seater was sighted which made no attempt to approach the Allied formation, but minutes later a mixed batch of Albatros single and two-seaters appeared, coming up fast on the south side of the Sopwiths.

Leaving Knaggs and Maxwell to cover the photo aircraft, Ball dived at full power towards the Albatri and, as he got within range of the leading machine, opened fire with both guns. His Vickers immediately jammed but he managed to get off half a drum of Lewis. The Germans

The last photo taken of Albert Ball, seated in SE5, A4850, on 6th May 1917

quickly swung away and retreated eastwards, re-forming at a safe distance and continuing to remain within striking range. Ball climbed and rejoined his companions. The Albatros formation continued to trail behind but despite several attempts by the SE5s to engage them, remained well out of range until reaching the lines, at which point they gave up the chase and returned eastwards.

Whilst Ball was away Major Blomfield spent an hour consulting with Major E R Pretyman, commander of 19 Squadron at Savy. Orders from Wing headquarters to Blomfield had detailed him to provide an offensive patrol in strength that evening; its object to seek out the stiffening German fighter opposition along the Arras front. Blomfield arranged with Pretyman to provide a section of 19 Squadron's Spad S7s to overlap his own SEW patrol area.

Though the heyday of the German fighter 'circus' was yet to come, the practice of grouping several *Jagdstaffeln* temporarily in one tactical fighting force had already produced moderate success; and opposing 56 Squadron at that time was one such group, comprised of *Jagdstaffeln* 3, 4, 11 and 33. Between them these four units included some of the most prominent German fighter pilots of the period; in particular *Jagdstaffel* 11 which was commanded by *Rittmeister* Manfred von Richthofen, destined to become Germany's 'Ace of Aces' before his death the following year.

By mid-afternoon all details for the proposed offensive 'sweep' had been arranged. The patrol was detailed to scour the sky above the Cambrai-Douai area, east of Lens, principally. Eleven SE5s of 56 Squadron would comprise the main hunting formation, while 19 Squadron was to despatch seven Spads to cover the fringes of the patrol zone. In addition a formation of Sopwith Triplanes from 8 Squadron RNAS would be airborne in the same general area at approximately the same period. The 56 Squadron formation was drawn from all three Flights, under the nominal leadership of Ball, and consisted of the following men and machines:

A Flight
Capt A Ball, DSO, MC	SE5, A4850
Lt G C Maxwell	SE5, A8902
Lt K J Knaggs	SE5, A8904

B Flight
Capt C M Crowe	SE5, A4860
Lt R M C Musters	SE5, A4867
Lt A P F Rhys-Davids	SE5, A4868
Lt J O Leach, MC	SE5, A4856

C Flight
Capt H Meintjes	SE5, A8900
Lt R T C Hoidge	SE5, A4862
Lt C A Lewis, MC	SE5, A4853
Lt W B Melville	SE5, A4861

Captain Arthur P F Rhys-Davids, DSO, MC,
56 Squadron

At 5.30pm Ball led the other ten SE5s off from Vert Galand,

> ...eleven chocolate-coloured, lean, noisy bullets, lifting, swaying, turning, rising, into formation – two fours and a three – circling and climbing steadily away towards the lines... the May evening is heavy with threatening masses of cumulus cloud, majestic skyscapes, solid-looking as snow mountains, fraught with caves and valleys, rifts and ravines...*

OPPOSITE: *2nd Lt K J Knaggs who flew with Ball on 7th May 1917*

* *Sagittarius Rising*, C A Lewis.

By the time the lines were reached the SEs were at 7,000 feet, and Ball led them across south of the Cambrai-Bapaume road, heading towards the northern edge of shell-shattered Cambrai. Within minutes a C Flight machine, Melville's, swung away from the formation, turning for home, with its engine spluttering and clanking – the latest victim of the fractious Hispano-Suiza engines of 56 Squadron. Ball, accompanied by Knaggs, continued into enemy territory at 7,000 feet, while Crowe and Meintjes took their men higher to 9,000, the whole force heading still towards Cambrai.

Over Bois-sous-Bourlon Crowe's B Flight entered some heavy cloud banks, but on emerging into clear sky again, Crowe realised that Roger Musters was no longer behind him. Only Arthur Rhys-Davids had noticed Musters leave the formation just before it entered the cloud bank; his SE dropping 500 feet in a wide curve, apparently intent on attacking a solitary aircraft below. Musters was never seen again, and was subsequently named as a victim of *Vizefeldwebel* Karl Menckhoff of *Jagdstaffel* 3. Crowe continued northwards, but in the meantime a third SE was about to leave the force. Gerald Maxwell had lost contact with his fellows in the layered clouds, and after a fruitless search eventually turned back to Vert Galand.

Apart from Musters' apparent combat, the first clash with enemy aircraft came when C Flight, led by 'Duke' Meintjes, spotted a white vee-strutter scout some 500 feet below them. Meintjes promptly led his men down in line astern to attack, and the German was riddled in turn by all four SEs, and fell away 'scuttled' (*sic*).

Climbing and regaining a loose formation, the SEs headed north-west over the Cambrai-Douai road, only to be surprised by four red-painted Albatros DIII Scouts, which appeared abruptly from a cloud on their own level. Although German records for this date are now sparse and incomplete, even to an extent confusing; there seems little doubt that these particular Albatros Scouts were one Kette (sub-Flight) of *Jagdstaffel* 11. The *Staffelführer*, Manfred von Richthofen, was on leave in Germany, and in his absence temporary command of the unit was in the capable hands of his younger brother, Lothar von Richthofen. The pilots of this German quartet were Lothar, Wilhelm Allmenröder, Eberhardt Mohnicke, and either Georg Simon or *Leutnant* Esser.

The SE5s immediately engaged the Albatri. Cecil Lewis dived on the nearest, putting a good burst of 50 rounds into its tail section as he banked round behind it, but the German pilot was no novice and had soon reversed the position getting onto Lewis's tail as the latter climbed steeply away. Meintjes tackled a second Albatros which promptly curved round onto the SE's tail and, despite Meintjes' violent manoeuvring, could not be shaken off.

Albatros D.III, 2015/16 of Jadgstaffel *11, piloted by* Lt *Georg Simon. Seen here after capture on 20th June 1917 at Dunkirk RNAS Depot in remarked insignia. The band around the fuselage is green.*

Slamming his rudder bar, the South African jerked his SE into a vertical bank, and then dropped into a fast corkscrew spin. His swift countermove proved successful and he finally lost his adversary. Climbing again, Meintjes saw a lone red Albatros at 9,000 feet and soon got behind it, closing to 50 yards distance and firing crisp bursts from his Vickers. As the German twisted and turned to evade his attacker, Meintjes closed to 25 yards and hammered in further bursts of Vickers. The German, *Leutnant* Wolfgang von Pluschow from *Jagdstaffel* 11, spun down and eventually crash-landed east of Gouy-sous-Bellone, receiving serious injuries.

Cecil Lewis, meantime continued climbing out of the general melee until he reached 12,000 feet; only to be immediately set upon by two more German scouts. Wrenching his SE into a fast dive, Lewis spun round and twisted down trying to shake off his latest opponents in vain, and was only saved from possible destruction by the timely intervention of K J Knaggs who suddenly appeared and engaged both Albatri with brief opening bursts from his Vickers.

As the two Germans veered away from this unexpected onslaught, Knaggs closed with one and continued to press his attack and both combatants were quickly lost to Lewis's view; climbing and still fighting into an overhead cloud. Knaggs and Ball had also met four red Albatros Scouts, a second *Kette* of *Jagdstaffel* 11 roaming the sky just then, and both SE5s dived to engage.

Ball, in the lead, commenced firing as he neared one Albatros but suddenly pulled away, possibly with a recurrence of the Vickers gun trouble he had earlier in the day. Knaggs selected a second Albatros as his target, getting to within 150 yards and firing steadily until his Vickers gun juddered to a stop.

Banking away, Knaggs remedied the stoppage and was about to resume his attack when he noticed Cecil Lewis' predicament. Abandoning his intended victim, Knaggs tackled both Germans, firing his Vickers in continuous bursts until the gun's trigger bar ruptured. Climbing up under one Albatros, Knaggs brought his wing-mounted Lewis gun into play until the German finally cleared east.

The SE5 continued climbing while Knaggs attempted to clear his Vickers gun, noticing at the same time 'reinforcements' in the shape of three Bristol Fighters from 48 Squadron and five or six Nieuport Scouts hurrying over to join the wheeling dogfight. Once his gun was working again, Knaggs spotted Ball below, alone, and dropped down to formate on Ball's side to resume their patrol. Lewis, after his 'rescue', climbed once more to 12,000 feet, where he met Reginald Hoidge and paired with him, searching for other SE5s.

'Duke' Meintjes, fresh from his success in downing von Pluschow, had climbed for fighting height, going north-west in the direction of Lens, when he noticed a lone red Albatros Scout just east of Lens, below him. Meintjes dived in to attack but the German had obviously seen his approach and had also commenced climbing for precious height as 'Duke' bore in to close range and started firing.

The German pilot evaded Meintjes' first attack, and quickly started the usual pattern of circling to position himself on his opponent's tail. As both men manoeuvred for a killing position, the German suddenly pulled into a tight reversing bank and fired an accurate burst through the SE5's cockpit. His bullets ripped through the side fabric, slashed through Meintjes' right wrist, and shattered the top of the SE's control column. Momentarily stunned by pain and shock, Meintjes let go his 'joystick' and the SE fell away, spinning slowly.

As it neared the ground Meintjes fought off his faintness, gathered his remaining strength and managed to bring the crippled SE5 down intact to land close to Sains-en-Gohelle. As the aircraft rolled to a stop Meintjes lapsed into unconsciousness, but fortuitously he had come to earth close to the headquarters of the 46th Division, and gentle hands soon lifted the wounded pilot out of his shattered cockpit and bore him away to a nearby field hospital.

Hoidge, who had joined Meintjes and the other C Flight men in the initial attack on a white Albatros, later dived on a pair of red Albatri, closing to within 25 yards of one and pouring in short bursts from his Vickers. The Albatros dropped its nose and dived, but Hoidge followed it down to 4,000 feet still firing as his target swam into his Aldis sight. The German continued spinning down until according to Hoidge's report, it 'spun into the ground' (*sic*), north-east of Cambrai.

Climbing westwards to 7,000 feet Hoidge then saw what he took to be five Nieuport Scouts and hurried to join their formation. When within 500 yards however he realised with a jolt that his 'Nieuports' were green-doped Albatros Scouts! All five set upon the lone SE5 and

Captain R T C Hoidge in SE5, A4862, at London Colney, April 1917

Hoidge had little option but to dive away westwards at all possible speed, jinking and twisting desperately as five pairs of German guns kept up a barrage of fire behind him.

Finally, and thankfully, losing his pursuers, Hoidge climbed back to 12,000 feet where he met Cecil Lewis over Arras, and the two resumed their patrol. Shortly afterwards Lewis spotted two SE5s a thousand feet below – Albert Ball and Knaggs – and, remaining at their relative altitudes, all four continued to scour the air above Vitry and the Lens-Arras-Douai roads.

By then, 7pm, visibility was deteriorating badly as storm clouds gathered and a beating drizzle of rain began to pelt against the aircraft. Lewis soon lost sight of Ball and Knaggs and, in view of their diminishing petrol states, he and Hoidge finally turned towards the lines and flew back to Vert Galand, landing there just before 8pm.

Cyril Crowe, leading the remaining two SE5s of B Flight after Musters' disappearance, travelled northwards and finally emerged from the cloud layers above the Sauchy-Lestrees station, near the Arras-Cambrai road. At once Crowe saw an Albatros Scout, its wings a bright green with a long red tail section, flying alone at 8,000 feet south of Vitry. With John Leach tucked in close behind him, Crowe dived at the Albatros getting in accurate Vickers gun fire at close range. The German went into a steep dive and, as Crowe overshot, Leach followed up with a close-range attack. Crowe angled in again but was frustrated by having a jam in his Vickers. Leach then fastened on the tail of the Albatros and blasted it with both guns from point blank range. The German scout continued its dive – 'completely scuttled', as the SE pilots later reported – to land near Gavrelle, east of Vitry.

The third member of Crowe's formation, Rhys-Davids, had been about to join Crowe and Leach in their initial dive on the green-red Albatros when he saw a second Albatros approaching from the direction of Douai. Before Rhys-Davids could decide what to do, the new-comer had curved behind him and started a series of short dive and climb attacks, firing brief and accurate bursts of fire – a sure sign of an experienced fighter pilot.

Within seconds the 19-years-old ex-Etonian was in serious trouble. His SE was riddled, its engine badly hit and leaking water coolant, and its undercarriage and wings splintered and torn by the German's deadly fire. To add to his predicament Rhys-Davids soon found that he was unable to defend himself – both of his guns were jammed. Remarkably cool in the face of his peril, the young SE pilot was considering how best to extricate himself from almost certain destruction when, for no obvious reason, the aggressive German left him abruptly and flew east, clearing the combat area.

Rhys-Davids, with a badly running engine, eased his stricken machine westwards to regain the safety of Allied territory, but two miles west of Arras his engine shuddered to a complete stop. Stretching his glide as flatly as possible, Rhys-Davids still hoped to reach Bellevue aerodrome, but was finally forced to land in a field close to Laherliers, base for 48 Squadron's Bristol Fighters. In his report later Rhys-Davids described his extremely skilled opponent as, 'Fuselage and tail painted bright red, with green band behind pilot's seat. Wings painted red and green. Very large red boss on propeller and very narrow tail plane. Wings slightly swept back.'

In retrospect, it is a tribute to the boy's coolness under fire in virtually his first serious air combat that his brain could absorb so much clinical detail about a machine that was ostensibly about to kill him. The identity of this particular German pilot is still unestablished. Several accounts by aviation writers in recent years have stated (with what evidence is not clear) that he was *Leutnant* Kurt Wolff of *Jagdstaffel* 11, one of Germany's leading fighter pilots at that date.

However, Wolff was not with his usual *Staffel* on May 7th, having been detached to the Champagne area

Jagdstaffel *11, 23rd April 1917, marking the 100th claimed victory for the unit. (L-R): Wilhelm Allmenröder, Hintsch, Sebastian Festner, Karl Schäfer, Manfred von Richthofen (in cockpit), Kurt Wolff (in front of Richthofen), Simon, Brauneck. Seated: Esser, Lothar von Richthofen, Krefft. At least four of these fought 56 Squadron on 7th May 1917*

of fighting on May 2nd to take temporary command of *Jagdstaffel* 29, and he did not return to his unit until May 9th.*

While Rhys-Davids was nursing his battered aircraft towards the lines, Cyril Crowe, having helped Leach to dispose of one Albatros, climbed and attacked another HA (hostile aircraft) from underneath with his Lewis gun, but his target vanished into clouds near Douai leaving Crowe with a clear sky around him for the moment.

* A much more likely pilot was *Leutnant* Georg Simon, who at this period was flying Albatros DIII, 2015/16 with *Jagdstaffel* 11, and was brought down in British lines on May 20th, 1917 by Lieutenant G Chapman, 29 Squadron, RFC and made a prisoner. His aircraft was doped red and green on its wings, had a red fuselage, with a broad green band round the fuselage just behind the cockpit. If indeed Simon was piloting this Albatros that evening, he would most probably have been Rhys-Davids' opponent.

Prior to take-off Ball had instructed all pilots to re-form east of Arras at 10,000 feet should the formation get scattered in individual fights; and Crowe now made towards Lecluse and then circled for a time hoping others would keep the prearranged rendezvous. In the event only one other SE5 arrived. The two men attempted to attack a two-seater over Beaumont at 8,000 feet, but their prey eluded them by diving steeply towards Douai. Turning back to Arras, the SEs were met by an Albatros Scout who immediately made for Crowe in a head-on attack.

As the two were on the point of colliding, Crowe zoomed over the top of the German, banked swiftly to get onto its tail, and missed death by a hairs-breadth as the German's bullets sliced the elastic holding band of his eye goggles and shot them away into the slipstream. By the time, only seconds later, that Crowe recovered from this shock, his late opponent was nowhere to be seen.

Climbing slightly, Crowe saw an enemy formation some 500 feet higher going towards Lens, and these quickly came piling down to attack him. Crowe fled to the west and finally outpaced them, then resumed his main patrol over Fresnoy. His late companion, John Leach was not so lucky. Tackling a lone Albatros (possibly Crowe's last opponent of the eye-goggles incident), Leach found himself outclassed by his more experienced adversary.

Within a minute Leach was falling to earth in a bullet-riven SE5, with one leg almost severed by a particularly accurate burst from the German. Near fainting from loss of blood and the waves of initial shock, Leach somehow got his machine down safely, landing between Gouy and Ablain St Nazaire, near No 4 Canadian Divisional Hospital. Still critically ill the following day, Leach was unable to give any account of his own part in that fateful evening patrol, and later suffered amputation of his smashed leg.

As Crowe continued to circle above Fresnoy he met Albert Ball coming straight through the fading light towards Lens, and turned to follow him. Suddenly from

Ball's cockpit two red Very lights etched crimson arcs against the glowering clouds – the signal for sighting enemy aircraft. Crowe searched the air around him but could see no other machines, and therefore continued to follow Ball. As they neared Loos Ball began a diving attack on a solitary red Albatros DIII below, and Crowe saw the lines of Buckingham tracers spurt from Ball's gun towards the German.

Following down, Crowe closed to 30-40 yards and fired a good burst before over-shooting his target. As he turned he saw Ball attacking again, and at that moment noticed two aircraft about 500 feet above – a Sopwith Triplane and a Spad S7 (Flight Lieutenant Reginald Soar, 8 (Naval) Squadron and Lieutenant R M Child, 19 Squadron respectively).

Below him Crowe saw that Ball was still engaged fighting the red Albatros and he continued to watch them as both aircraft disappeared into a dark grey cumulus cloud, still firing and fighting, flying due east. Scouting round the cloud pillar, Crowe could not find the two aircraft in the rapidly darkening sky. Just below him, however, was an enemy two-seater and Crowe dived to attack. The German crew promptly fled eastwards in a steep dive and soon was lost to sight. Checking his fuel gauges, Crowe realised it was time to return and accordingly flew south to Lens and eventually landed at Auchel airfield at about 8.15pm, his petrol tanks dry.

As Cyril Crowe eased his SE5 down onto the grass landing strip at Auchel, Albert Ball was flying low over rough ground near Seclin village, heading westwards towards Annoeullin village, still pursuing the red Albatros that he and Crowe had attacked. Visibility was still bad and just before reaching Annoeullin the German turned in one last attempt to ward off his relentless hunter. Then, with a bullet ruptured petrol tank, the Albatros crash-landed. Its pilot, *Leutnant* Lothar von Richthofen, climbed out of his machine unharmed, in time to see the tail of Ball's SE5 disappear into thick cloud in a gentle climb.

The only German witnesses to what actually followed were four officers on the ground nearby; *Leutnant* Franz Hailer of *Flieger-Abteilung* A292, his brother Carl, and two companions. Hearing the sound of aircraft engines, Franz Hailer, through his field binoculars, saw Ball's SE5 emerge from low cloud, upside down, its propeller stopped, and trailing a thin plume of black, oily smoke, descending in a shallow dive. As Hailer continued to watch, the SE5 disappeared briefly behind a line of trees and almost immediately crashed, still inverted, into some slightly rising ground near a ruined farmhouse called Fashoda, just over a mile from the village of Annoeullin.

Hailer and his three companions immediately hurried to the site of the crash, to find Ball's body had already

Carl and Franz Hailer of Flieger-Abteilung *9b in front of an AGO C.1*

been removed from the wreckage of his machine and laid on the ground nearby by a local French girl. The girl, Madame Lieppe-Coulon, had been first to reach the wrecked aircraft, and after seeing that Ball was apparently still breathing, had lifted him gently from his fractured cockpit. Ball, cradled in her arms, lived only for a few seconds; his eyes opened just once.

From various personal items in Ball's uniform, Hailer was able to identify him as Albert Ball, a name well-known to the Germans – 'We called him the English Richthofen' – and after a cursory examination of Ball himself, Hailer was positive that the boy had not been wounded in any way; his various injuries had all been

Mme Lieppe-Coulon, taken in 1911 when she was 16 years old

sustained in the crash. Ball's face and head were unmarked, though later some slight bruising of the cheek became apparent, doubtless the result of Ball hitting his face against the cockpit rim on impact.

Hailer arranged for Ball to be taken to the nearest field hospital, where a German doctor examined him more thoroughly to ascertain the actual cause of death. His report confirmed Hailer's opinion that there were no battle wounds. In the doctor's expert opinion Ball's death had been due simply to his crash injuries, which included a broken back, crushing of the chest and one broken arm; three fractures of the left leg and foot; and several minor abrasions generally.

That evening Ball was placed in the hospital 'chapel', an appropriately furnished field tent, to be prepared for burial. Hailer returned to his unit and suggested to his unit commander that Ball's body should be wrapped in a flag and dropped by parachute behind British lines '...so that his comrades could bury him with the honour due to

BELOW AND OPPOSITE: *Funeral of Albert Ball, attended by senior German officers and officials and some Allied prisoners of war*

him.' Hailer's chivalrous thought was not acceptable to German higher authority.

From the SE5's wreckage and from Ball's uniform a small collection of personal belongings were gathered together. A thin gold wrist identity bracelet; a white cambric handkerchief, initialled A in one corner; the little book of prayers which Flora Young had given Ball just before he left England for the last time; a pocket penknife; fountain pen; two pencils; and a £1 Treasury note. Other 'souvenirs' removed included a small, crumpled, silver cigarette case; a compass; and the RFC 'wings' and medal ribbons sewn on his tunic. Of these, Franz Hailer handed the wrist bracelet to his unit commander, but privately retained the handkerchief and prayer book.

On May 9th Albert Ball was buried in a wooden coffin, a rare mark of respect in the front-line fighting zones, and given a military funeral with honours in the Annoeullin village cemetery. In attendance were various representatives of nearby German military units, some British prisoners of war, and a large crowd of local French residents. His grave, Plot No 999 in the contemporary site plan, was marked with a simple white wooden cross,

constructed and suitably inscribed by the carpenter of a
nearby German flying unit.

At Vert Galand airfield that evening Major Blomfield
and the crews of 56 Squadron waited glumly. Of the
eleven SE5s which set out, only five had returned to base
by 8.30pm – Maxwell and Melville earlier; Lewis, Hoidge
and Knaggs later. Soon news was received that Crowe and
Rhys-Davids were down in British lines, safe and
unharmed. But by midnight there was still no news of
Ball, Musters or Meintjes; and only sad news of John
Leach, critically ill in a hospital.

At first the men of 56 simply could not accept that Ball
might be dead; to all of them he had seemed invincible. Yet
privately several of the more experienced pilots
instinctively felt he must be. Ball's methods of fighting,
tackling all and any odds head-on, day after day, virtually
without pause, could only have one, inevitable conclusion.
The only hope possible that he was forced down and had
become a prisoner of war was equally feasible. Ball's
consistent habit of fighting until he was out of ammunition,
and dangerously low on fuel, had often left him in a highly
vulnerable position, well behind enemy lines.

This thought offered, at least a faint hope that Ball was
still alive. The men of 56, air and ground crews, clung
desperately to that thought.

13

Sequel

THE circumstances surrounding and leading to Albert
Ball's death still remain unresolved completely. On
the German side official credit for a 'victory' was given to
Lothar von Richthofen. Filing a routine claim, Lothar
quoted the number of the wrecked SE5's Hispano-Suiza
engine positively, but identified the machine itself,
incorrectly, as a triplane, brought down at Annoeullin at
8.30pm on May 7th. In part his claim's narrative read:

> On May 7th I had a combat with many
> triplanes. One of them attacked me in a very
> determined manner. We fired a great deal at each
> other, and during the combat he came very close.
> He came down under my fire. My machine was
> damaged, and I landed with a dead propeller, near
> the hostile machine.

The many anomalies in the German 'evidence' for
Lothar's claim, not least of these being Lothar's own
statement, cast the gravest doubts as to the authenticity of
any 'victory'. While it is true that some Sopwith Triplanes
of 8 (Naval) Squadron had flown that evening on the
fringes of the sprawling succession of combats over
Cambrai and Arras, no triplane was lost (or even seriously
damaged) by the Allied air services on that day.

Lothar's statement that his opponent, '... came very
close' merely adds to the mystery of his claim for a
triplane. Lothar was an experienced operational fighter
pilot, already accredited with 16 combat victories, and
familiar with most Allied fighter designs in general. The
SE5, though a new design to most Germans at that time,

was nevertheless unmistakable as a biplane.

The final state of the SE5's wreckage is unknown precisely, though there is written evidence that a Saxon officer took photographs of the wreck privately; photos which have yet to be unearthed and authenticated. Several photographs purporting to be of Ball's final crash exist still – indeed, continue to be regarded as authentic – but objective scrutiny of these indicates that none have any connection with Ball.

Only one report, an unofficial one, gives any form of detailed description of the genuine wreckage, and this states quite positively that the SE5's complete tail section broke away from the fuselage on initial impact and was never found. If indeed this was the case it would, at least, explain Lothar von Richthofen's inability to quote the SE's serial number, A4850, which was doped only on the tail fin of the machine. Normally, such serial numbers were priority souvenirs to be cut from any victim's machine by the German fighter pilots.

Certain major items were extracted from the wreck and presented to Lothar as keepsakes, including the Vickers machine gun No A541, two Very pistols, part of the Vickers' ammunition belt, some instruments from the SE5's dashboard, and a small section of a petrol feed pipe slashed by a bullet scar. These items went to the Richthofen home at Schweidnitz where they were eventually mounted on the walls of one room devoted to the memory of Lothar after his death.

In 1944, when the Schweidnitz area was occupied by the Russian Army, the remaining members of the Richthofen family fled hurriedly to the west, leaving behind everything connected with the memorial displays to the Richthofen brothers; and, it was reported, the various items in the Schweidnitz home were transferred to the Moscow Air Museum.

As required by the contemporary German strict ruling for any combat victory claim, Lothar had to produce at

Lothar von Richthofen, credited officially with shooting down Albert Ball on 7th May 1917, but clear evidence denies any such claim

least three 'objective', confirmatory witnesses to attest to his claim. Four such 'witnesses' filed statements backing Lothar's claim. *Leutnant* Hepner of Kite Balloon *Abteilung Nr 1* 'Saw a triplane fall out of control': *Flakgruppe* 22 'Saw a triplane shot down'; Kite Balloon Section 22 'Saw English machine crash near Faschoda (*sic*) and saw German machine land near Bauvin'; and *Leutnant* Franz Hailer of *Flieger-Abteilung* A292 (already mentioned). Satisfied with such documentary confirmation, German higher authority duly credited Lothar von Richthofen with Ball's SE5 as the German's 17th *Luftsiege*.

The unlikely 'coincidence' of so many witnesses each, independently (?), mistaking a biplane for a triplane leaves great doubt as to the authenticity of certain of these statements. And it may be of no little significance that the official file covering the circumstances of Ball's death was placed in the German State Secret Archives, and remained there – unavailable to researchers – until early 1945 when the archives were, in the main, destroyed by Allied bombing.

Close examination of the SE5's wreckage by Franz Hailer and others revealed no evidence of it being brought down by either bullet or shell, though several isolated bullet holes and inconsequential damage had been sustained from, presumably, air combat.

Equally, Ball had suffered no wound from gun fire of any description; his death had been due solely to crash injuries, as witnessed by the German doctor's report of his examination shortly after Ball's body had been brought into the field hospital.

Hailer has also recorded that much later in the evening of May 7th he answered a telephone call to his unit from the adjutant of *Jagdstaffel* 11, who wished to know if any crashed British aircraft had been discovered in Hailer's locality, as the *Staffel's* pilots had put in claims for two British machines brought down. Hailer replied that one machine had been found, its pilot being the famous Captain

Ball, but that in his opinion this machine had not been brought down by aircraft or anti-aircraft fire. Hailer's commanding officer then took over the call, and nothing is known of what was said during the remaining conversation.

Whether Ball was actually responsible for shooting down Lothar von Richthofen's Albatros is impossible to establish. Apart from Ball, Cyril Crowe had also attacked Lothar just before the German and Ball disappeared into a cloudbank; while Lieutenant R M Child of 19 Squadron was also said to have fired at the same Albatros. What is beyond doubt is that Ball was piloting the SE5 which pursued the younger Richthofen during the final minutes before Lothar was forced to crash-land.

The original grave marker, made by Germans, on Ball's grave. Later given to Trent College and displayed in the college chapel.

The now unchallengeable evidence of Franz Hailer –
his three companions on that date were later killed, or
died – is adamant that Ball's aircraft finally emerged from
low cloud in an inverted flying attitude and then crashed.
It can only be speculation now as to how Ball came to be
in such a dangerous position, a mere 500 feet or less
above the ground. By that time, approximately 8.30pm,

*The second marker for Ball's grave, made by RAF
personnel of 207 Squadron in December 1918*

*The (now) permanent grave marker
(photo taken 1976)*

Ball had been airborne for three hours, had been engaged in several skirmishes with enemy machines, and must have been approaching the limit of his machine's fuel endurance. In addition, it would be reasonable to suppose that Ball, by then, was tired, mentally and physically, and possibly near-exhausted by three hours of constant vigilance and peaks of high nervous tension.

The theory has been propounded that, on entering cloud again after seeing Lothar von Richthofen's Albatros go to earth, Ball became disorientated, and only realised that he was not flying straight and level when he finally came out of the cloud, upside down and shallow-diving towards the ground. If indeed this was the case, and such a situation was wholly possible, then Ball, or any other pilot, would have had only the remotest chance of regaining a normal flying attitude in an SE5 at such a low altitude. The early production models of the SE5 had a tendency to flood their air intake and filters with petrol from the engine carburettor if flown anywhere near a vertical bank; and if inverted could seldom be flown for more than a few seconds without loss of control.

Once in an inverted attitude an early production SE5, such as Ball's A4850, would need time in which to restart its engine, even assuming that the machine was immediately recovered from its upside-down position. Necessarily, such a recovery required one paramount safety margin – plenty of height above the ground. Albert Ball had no such margin available to him.

At Vert Galand airfield that fateful evening the men of 56 Squadron waited in vain for some news or indication of the fate of Ball. On May 9th, assuming that at least he must be a prisoner of war, his Nieuport Scout, B1522, was flown by Cecil Lewis to the nearby RFC Depot for further disposal.*

---

* Nieuport 17, B1522, was later issued to 1 Squadron, RFC on June 6th 1917; and further re-issued to 29 Squadron, RFC on August 19th 1917. Three weeks later, on September 7th, it was returned to the RFC Depot as obsolete for front-line operations.

On May 12th, still without definite information of the missing pilots, 9th Wing RFC Headquarters authorised Major Blomfield to have officially prepared messages dropped behind the German lines, requesting news of Ball and Musters. Two days later Ball's father wrote to Blomfield, thanking him for his private notification that Albert was missing in action, and particularly requesting the return of Ball's personal diary and other private papers. In the continued absence of specific news, Ball was officially promulgated as 'Missing' on May 18th.

Only at the end of May, some three weeks after Ball's death, did the German authorities arrange for various messages to be dropped in British lines confirming his fate, and one of these stated briefly that he had been buried in Annoeullin. The news was immediately transmitted to the War Office in London, and then to Arthur Richardson, Member of Parliament for Nottingham; to whom fell the sad duty of personally breaking the news to Ball's family.

On June 8th 1917 the *London Gazette* announced the posthumous award of a Victoria Cross to Albert Ball; and notification was received that the President of France had appointed the Nottingham boy as a *Chevalier* of the *Legion d'Honneur*.

Nottingham's own tribute to their latest VC came on June 10th, when St Mary's Church was filled to capacity with a cross-section of people representing all sections of the local community, on the occasion of a memorial service for Ball. The glittering procession to the church had passed through densely packed crowds in the city centre, and was comprised of every local dignitary, association and society, with Service representatives from the Army and Royal Flying Corps; and including as chief mourners Ball's father and brother Cyril. Ball's mother, totally grief-stricken by her son's death, could not bring herself to attend. Lining the route of the procession were Boy Scouts of Albert's old troop and other local youth organisations.

Only hours after the official news of the boy's death was received in Nottingham, the city council held a meeting to pay its tribute of respect and sympathy to the memory of Ball; and at the same meeting first proposed that a fund be opened for subscriptions to a tangible memorial to him, possibly a marble statue, to be placed prominently within the precincts of the city. This fund for the proposed statue swelled daily with contributions from all quarters; ranging from a silver sixpenny piece from a small child – 'It took me six hours work in the garden to get, so I hope you will accept it', read the accompanying note – to large cheques from prominent business men and members of the local aristocracy. The subsequent tale of 'progress' on this projected memorial statue makes sad reading, however.

It was not until January 1919 that the sculptor was finally appointed, and contracts accepted for the work. A further

Albert Ball's Memorial Service procession in Nottingham on 12th June 1917. Cyril Ball (in RFC uniform) alongside his father.

Ball's parents receive their son's Victoria Cross from HM King George V at Buckingham Palace on 21st July 1917

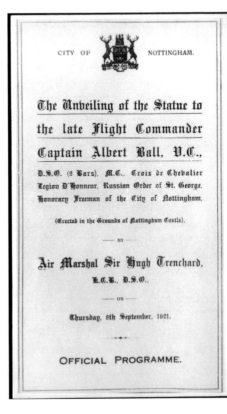

CITY OF   NOTTINGHAM.

The Unveiling of the Statue to the late Flight Commander Captain Albert Ball, V.C.,

D.S.O. (2 Bars), M.C., Croix de Chevalier Legion D'Honneur, Russian Order of St. George, Honorary Freeman of the City of Nottingham.

(Erected in the Grounds of Nottingham Castle).

— BY —

Air Marshal Sir Hugh Trenchard, K.C.B., D.S.O.,

— ON —

Thursday, 8th September, 1921.

OFFICIAL PROGRAMME.

Official programme cover for the unveiling of Ball's statue in the grounds of Nottingham Castle, 8th September 1921 eleven months elapsed before the statue and its base surround was declared completed. Further procrastination by the council in deciding on a location for the statue lasted ten months; and then the accounts department began receiving letters and invoices from the contractors, and sculptor, requesting their well-overdue payments.

After more months of delay, and much correspondence, the Nottingham civic leaders finally drew up a balance sheet of up-dated costs and outstanding debts connected with work on the statue, and received a shock! Despite the initial generosity of contributors to the memorial fund, the costings showed an overspending well in excess of £1,000. With the knowledge that the Prince of Wales had already been invited to perform the unveiling ceremony, the council members were in what can only be termed a 'panic situation'. Within 48 hours of the accountant's revelations, hand-written letters in fine copperplate script, marked 'Private and Confidential' and signed by the mayor, town clerk and chairman of the general purposes committee, were discreetly dispatched to all leaders of the city's industry and commerce. Referring to a 'difficult and delicate situation', the letters were bland, if diplomatic appeals for further contributions to cover the outstanding debts. Fortunately, the response in virtually every case was most generous, and the necessary monies forwarded, again discreetly in most cases.

Arrangements were put in hand for the unveiling of the statue with appropriate pomp and ceremony. It had finally been decided to locate the memorial in the grounds of Nottingham Castle, on a gentle slope beneath the walls, overlooking the heart of the city.

In the event, due to other commitments, the Prince of Wales was unable to accept the city's invitation to perform the ceremony; and instead Sir Hugh Trenchard, now Chief of the Air Staff, RAF, was invited for this duty. Trenchard willingly agreed to thus honour Ball, though not without distinct reservations on the original proposed arrangements and pre-publicity for the occasion. Trenchard made it plain that far too much emphasis appeared to be paid to his presence; whereas the real purpose of the ceremony was to honour Ball. His wishes were heeded, and on September 8th 1921 came the end of the statue 'saga'; when Hugh Trenchard, in the presence of Ball's family and a huge gathering of local citizens, unveiled the memorial statue in the grounds of Nottingham Castle, where it stands today.

After the war Ball's father journeyed to France to locate his son's grave, and to ascertain as best he could the circumstances of Albert's death. Purchasing the field in which Ball had crashed, the father had a plain memorial stone erected on the spot where Ball's SE5 met its end, and where Ball had breathed his last, cradled in the arms of a local French girl.

The unveiling of Ball's statue in the grounds of Nottingham Castle, 8th September 1921. At rear: Air Marshal Hugh Trenchard, Alderman H Bowles, Cllr J M Frecklingham. In front: Ball's parents

He also visited the cemetery at Annoeullin village, and subsequently replaced the temporary wooden cross placed there by members of 207 Squadron RAF in 1919 by a marble headstone and surround. For the constant maintenance of the grave and its surrounds, he invested a sum of money in perpetuity – a fund which continues for this purpose to the present day. Several years after the father's visit to France, and the various arrangements he made, moves were made – in part by officials of the Imperial War Graves Commission, and partly by the then parliamentary member for South Nottingham – to have Ball's body reinterred in his home town.

In the event Ball's father would not agree to such a move, and Albert Ball remains where he was buried originally, in Grave No 643 of the German extension of Annoeullin Communal Cemetery, the only Englishman

The refurbished stone marking the place where Ball died on 7th May 1917

among a host of black-crossed grave markers of his former enemies.

Today, there remains an impressive host of relics and memorabilia of Albert Ball. Appropriately, the Nottingham Castle Museum reserves a special corner for the display of Ball's complete medals and awards, photographs and various personal items. London's Imperial War Museum displays a tunic, and scraps from his crashed SE5 A4850. In the May Hall of his old school, Trent College, pride of place is given to the original oil painting made of Ball by Denholm Davies – loaned to the college by Ball's sister, Mrs Lois B Anderson – while in the pupils' dining room hangs a propeller from one of Ball's Nieuport Scouts. In the Trent College chapel hangs the first wooden marker cross erected over Ball's grave in 1917 by the Germans.

Nor is he forgotten by the present generations of RAF men; in the crew room of 56 Squadron RAF (at the time of writing, 1976), prominently displayed, is one of Ball's complete Royal Flying Corps uniforms, and a variety of photographs and paintings; also, still in constant working use, is a clock mounted in the hub of his SE5 A4850's propeller, which was presented to 56 Squadron by Ball's father just over 40 years ago.

In the Royal Air Force Museum at Hendon, near London, where Ball first learned to fly, can be found several small, personal items recovered from Ball's body by some unknown German and eventually returned to his family. Elsewhere, privately treasured by members or relatives of Ball's family, are many other mementoes, each a tangible link with the smiling boy whom each individual loved in his or her own way.

In 1967, coinciding with the 50th anniversary of his death, Ball's memory was further perpetuated by Trent College with the inception of the *Albert Ball, VC Scholarships*. Commencing in September 1967, the governors of the college agreed to accept a certain number of day-attendance boys, aged between 12 and 16 years,

Ball's statue, looking out over Nottingham City

who were adjudged worthy of this privilege. Initially two such scholarships were to be awarded each year.

That one boy should be so extensively remembered and honoured among the many who were sacrificed during the 1914-18 holocaust – he was but one of nearly 8,000 airmen killed in the British air services alone – may seem invidious. Perhaps what marks Albert Ball apart is the wholly unconscious example of splendid courage, devotion to an ideal of duty, and untarnished honour set by the 20-years-old Nottingham boy. He inspired a generation of fellow fliers in his lifetime, and enriched an already glittering tradition of service and duty for later generations of Royal Air Force men to inherit and embellish. Perhaps his most fitting epitaph are the words of another Royal Flying Corps pilot, the late Duncan Grinnel-Milne. After a spell as a prisoner of the Germans, Grinnel-Milne escaped from his captivity and returned to England, from where, in 1918, he was posted to 56 Squadron in France. His introduction to the unit by a friend was, 'You're in luck to be sent here. This is the most famous scout squadron in France. Ball was in it ...' Grinnel-Milne continued:

> I thought of a dark, stone-vaulted room in a German prison, and of a Scottish pilot recently captured telling me of the squadrons and airmen in France... and the best of the bunch, Captain Ball.*

* *Wind in the Wires*, D Grinnel-Milne.

14

'They shall grow not old…'

THE death of Albert Ball was mourned throughout the British nation. Long obituaries appeared in journals and newspapers throughout the world, each waxing loquaciously upon his great fighting career and combat prowess, emphasising the 'boy warrior' aspect of his international reputation.

To his mother, however, Albert's death was solely a shatteringly abrupt loss of a dearly beloved son; of a gentle boy who had not even attained his majority. The effect on her gentle soul was devastating. From the moment Harriet Ball received the dreaded news that her eldest boy was 'Missing in action', she was grief-stricken with anxiety; and the eventual confirmation of his death prostrated her, to the extent that she was unable to face the ordeal of attending the public memorial service held in Nottingham for Albert. Less than a year later a second blow to her was the official notification that her other son, Cyril, was 'Missing', and for a few anxious weeks she became virtually inconsolable, until the news filtered through that Cyril was alive and well as a prisoner of war in Germany.

These traumatic shocks almost certainly shortened her life. During the remaining years left to her, the circumstances of Albert's death were never mentioned in her presence; she clung instead to the loving memory of her son as he was in life – joyful, ebullient amongst his intimate friends, devoted to his mother and family. Albert's mother to all intents withdrew from her previously normal social scene, and when her husband was knighted in January 1924, and she became Lady Ball, continued to prefer the confines of her immediate family and closest friends rather than the usual social whirl. Lady

Ball never quite recovered from the loss of Albert, and on March 25th 1931, she died, still grieving for him.

Albert's younger brother Cyril, who had joined the Sherwood Foresters once he was of age, transferred to the Royal Flying Corps to train as a pilot. In December 1917 he was posted to France for active service, and joined his brother's old unit, 60 Squadron, based then at St Marie Cappel, flying SE5As, where he was allotted to A Flight. His Flight commander, Captain R L Chidlaw-Roberts, MC,

Lt Cyril Ball at Roulers on 5th February 1918 after being forced to land in German territory by Otto Esswein of Jagdstaffel 26

said of Cyril, 'He thought he could carry on like his brother. He was wrong, though full of guts.' Undoubtedly Cyril Ball felt that as Albert's brother he had a reputation to live up to, indeed, throughout his life he inevitably suffered 'comparisons' with his elder, famous brother, and at times part-resented the continuous comparison.

His fighting career with 60 Squadron lasted only a few weeks. On February 5th 1918 he flew SE5A B533 as part of a fighting patrol deep into German-held territory, and his engine was hit by a stray sliver of shell from some desultory anti-aircraft fire. With a dead engine, Cyril turned for home, but at that moment the patrol was jumped by Albatros DV scouts from *Jagdstaffel* 26, and Cyril was singled out for attack by the veteran *Leutnant* Otto Esswein. With no alternative open to him, Cyril was forced to land and become a captive of some local German troops. That day he was entertained briefly by the pilots of *Jagdstaffel* 26, and was then whisked away to a prisoner of war camp for the remaining months of the war.

In December 1918, Cyril was repatriated to England, and returned to his home in Nottingham, where he married his fiancée, Marie Prince, and commenced in business with his brother's old firm, the Universal Engineering Company in Castle Boulevard.

Cyril maintained his interest in aviation to the extent of flying with the local flying club, the Nottingham Aero Club at Hucknall aerodrome. Unlike his father, Cyril had little real ambition in the field of politics, and it was not until November 1947 that he became a city councillor for the Meadows Ward of Nottingham, and was re-elected for the years 1951–54. Only four years later, on July 2nd 1958, Cyril Ball died in the Nottingham General Hospital after a brief illness.

Throughout his life Albert Ball's father seldom overlooked any opportunity to perpetuate the memory of his eldest son. As Cyril Ball once remarked, 'Albert, my brother, hated any kind of show at all. My father loved it;

he liked being the father of England's first real ace.' Even allowing for Cyril's possible feelings of slight resentment at what he might have considered a form of 'favouritism' shown to his brother, his remark could be taken as a succinct summation of the elder Ball's consistent attempts to perpetuate his son's name and fame.

Complete RFC uniform of Albert Ball held in custody in 1976 by No 56 Squadron RAF

During his postwar visits to France, the father first established the precise location of the spot where Albert's aircraft had crashed, and immediately purchased the field in which this had occurred. On the exact spot of the crash he then had erected a stone marker plaque, inscribed,

> To the loving memory of Captain Albert Ball, VC, DSO, Two Bars, MC, Croix de Chevalier Legion d'Honneur, Order of Saint George, Russia, Hon Freeman of the City of Nottingham. One of England's Famous Airmen who fell on this spot fighting gloriously May 7th,1917. Aged 20 years.

In the same field he had a second stone marker raised, inscribed, 'This plot of land is given for the use of French soldiers by Sir Albert Ball on condition that this stone is protected.' Finally, he had a path laid from the spot where his son had died to the nearby roadway, the route over which Albert's body had travelled when being taken from the aircraft wreck to the German field hospital.

Seeking details of the actual cause of his son's death, the father interviewed a Belgian nurse who claimed to have been working in the German hospital to which Albert's body was taken and medically examined immediately after the crash. For reasons, and with what evidence, still unknown, this nurse told the father that Albert Ball had died as a result of a heart attack just prior to crashing. Ball's father chose firmly to believe her, and subsequently refuted any other explanation offered, despite the (then) available medical evidence of the true causes of death. It would be merely impertinent speculation to attempt any explanation of the father's adamant refusal to accept the unequivocal factual details; only he could really have known his reasons for his somewhat illogical decision.

Other 'memorials' to his son included the Eccentric Club Hostel at 4 King Edward's Road, Hackney in London, which was a hostel for disabled ex-Servicemen opened in July 1917 and dedicated to Albert Ball. On September 7th 1922, the Albert Ball Memorial Homes were officially declared open in Lenton village, near Nottingham; located at the rear of the Lenton War Memorial which had been erected in 1919. Several other perpetuations of the Ball family names in general, and young Albert in particular, can be seen today in Lenton and the vicinity.

In June 1933, Sir Albert re-married, taking as his second wife the former Estelle Dannah, from Quorn in Leicestershire – now (1976), Lady Estelle Shrigley-Ball. In September of the same year, a third biography of his son was published; *Captain Albert Ball, vc, dso* by John Hamilton Ltd, written by a Birmingham history master, R H Kiernan. In the book, Kiernan pointed to the semi-legend unwittingly created by the original Victoria Cross citation which stated that Ball had destroyed a total of 43 German aircraft and one kite balloon; then, quite objectively, explained the actual results of Ball's many combat 'victories'.

Sir Albert Ball, before seeing a copy of the book, and apparently solely on the basis of an unsigned review of the book in a national newspaper, immediately threatened both author and publisher with a legal suit to have the book withdrawn. In a newspaper interview (*Manchester Evening News*, dated September 28th, 1933) he is quoted as saying (in part):

> This book must be stopped. I will not stand by and see my dead son attacked in this way … I think the statements in the book are a slur, not only on my son, but on the whole Royal Flying Corps and the Royal Air Force. It is a slur I will fight.

In the event nothing further occurred – presumably in the interim Sir Albert had read the book on his solicitor's advice, and realised that Kiernan's account was not only plainly objective on the matter of Ball's victories, but almost entirely in praise of the boy. Certainly, Kiernan himself heard no more of the threatened legal suit. From 1936-37, Sir Albert Ball served his fourth term as Mayor of Nottingham – the office being retitled as Lord Mayor from 1927 – and, indeed, continued to play an active part in civic and social affairs until his death on March 27th 1946.

Albert's sister Lois – 'Dearest Lol', as he had always called her in his many letters home – married Lieutenant George S Anderson on March 2nd 1918, and two of her bridesmaids were Marie Prince, Cyril's fiancée, and Flora Young. The couple had two children; Cynthia, and a boy whom they named Albert. The son, by a curious coincidence, joined the Royal Air Force eventually and in 1940-41 was trained as a fighter pilot. By early 1943 he was a pilot with the famed 74 'Tiger' Squadron, flying Spitfire Vbs from the airfield at Nicosia, Cyprus. In September 1943, the German forces started a massive offensive in the area, and Flight Lieutenant Albert

Flt Lt Albert Anderson RAF, son of Lois Anderson, née Ball and nephew of Albert Ball

Anderson was one of nine Spitfires of 74 Squadron which set out from Nicosia on the 27th to counter some strong Luftwaffe bomber formations attacking Allied troops on the island of Kos. Ten miles south-east of Castelrosso, his engine gave serious trouble and Anderson was forced to bale out but, being only 500 feet above the sea, his parachute had no time to deploy fully. A high speed launch from Castelrosso and air-sea rescue aircraft from Cyprus made intensive searches, but Flight Lieutenant Albert Anderson, nephew of Albert Ball, was never found. It was a tragic quirk of fate that Lois should have to bear the same form of grief as her mother – the loss in aerial warfare of a dearly loved son.

What of the men who fought alongside Albert Ball in the years 1916-17? Some, perhaps inevitably, shared Ball's fate; a brief, brilliant fighting career and then death in the skies over Europe. One such was Arthur Rhys-Davids, ex-Captain of Eton and a classics scholar whose first real baptism of fire came in the evening that Ball died. Soon regarded on 56 Squadron as a 'second Ball', he swiftly built up a reputation for splendid courage, tackling all odds and ever eager to join combat. In six months of fighting Rhys-Davids ran up a tally of more than 20 victories, and was awarded a DSO and MC for his prowess.

On October 27th 1917 he was one of a 56 Squadron patrol over the German lines which sighted two German two-seaters and immediately gave chase, with Rhys-Davids as ever well to the fore. At almost the same moment the patrol was attacked by some Albatros Scouts, and Rhys-Davids was last seen still in pursuit of the two-seaters. He never returned, and was later reported by the Germans as having been killed in combat near Moeuvres.*
K L Knaggs, another member of Ball's ultimate patrol, and a great admirer of the Nottingham boy, was himself killed nearly a year later, on March 3rd 1918.

* Rhys-Davids was killed in action by *Leutnant* Karl Gallwitz of *Jasta* Boelcke.

Leslie Foot – known universally as 'Feet' – had been Ball's closest friend in 11, 60 and 56 Squadron. He ended the war safely and continued in peacetime with a career in civil aviation; joining the Handley Page Company initially, and then becoming a test pilot for the Bristol Aeroplane firm. On June 23rd 1923, Foot piloted the Bristol Monoplane M1D, G-EAVP in the Grosvenor Trophy Race, and set out from Filton to fly to Croydon. On his approach to Croydon one wing of the little monoplane tore away and the machine crashed near Chertsey and erupted in flames immediately, killing its pilot.

Ball's ultimate aerial opponent, Lothar von Richthofen, also survived the war and turned to civil aviation as a career. On July 14th 1922, piloting a passenger aircraft, Lothar ran into trouble near Hamburg when his engine ceased to function smoothly. Attempting to reach Fuhlsbüttel aerodrome, Lothar was on his final landing approach when his aircraft undercarriage hit some trees around the airfield boundary and dived into the ground. Lothar was dragged from the wreckage, but died on his way to hospital.

Some of Ball's contemporaries not only survived the war but then established successful careers, served throughout another world cataclysm in 1939-45 and eventually died peacefully. Reginald Hoidge, the Canadian, served in 56 Squadron with Ball, then in 1918 served in France again, with 1 Squadron; running up an accredited total of 26 victories and being awarded a Military Cross. He eventually died in 1963.

Cecil Lewis, the tall, slender boy who had fought alongside Ball on the fateful May evening of 1917, also survived the war, and then commenced a widely varying career. After a spell of flying with Vickers Aviation Ltd, Lewis became a flying instructor to the Chinese Government in Peking; and in the early 1920s was one of the four founder-members of the British Broadcasting Service (BBC) in the capacity of Chairman of the

Programme Board. His talents in the arts and literary
fields were exemplified by his many activities in the stage,
screen and television fields; whilst one book he wrote,
Sagittarius Rising, an account of his WWI experiences,
was published in 1936, and is still regarded as probably
the classic book on the subject of aerial warfare in 1914-
18. During the 1939-45 war, Lewis rejoined the RAF and
served for a long spell in the Air Ministry, before
resuming active service as a flying instructor, and finally
as commander of various staging posts in Sicily and
Greece. After the war, Cecil Lewis emigrated to South
Africa, and, typically, made the journey by air, flying a
tiny Miles Gemini aircraft.

Ball's commander in 11 Squadron in 1916, the gentle-
souled T O'Brien Hubbard, ended his war as a
Lieutenant-Colonel, MC, AFC, and remained in the Royal
Air Force. Promoted to Wing Commander in January
1922 Hubbard then served in Palestine and Transjordan;
returned to England to command the RAF station at
Bircham Newton in 1927, and, in September 1929,
returned to Iraq where he succeeded to command of the
RAF station at Hinaidi. From there he retired from the

Austin-Ball FB1, B9909...

RAF on September 13th 1931, after a total of 19 years service in the Army, RFC and RAF. As one brother officer wrote of him on his retirement from the service, 'A loved officer and a great gentleman...'

The commander of 8 Squadron RFC during Albert Ball's brief, imposed 'rest' in 1916 Patrick H L Playfair, also remained in the RAF as a permanent career, and rose to become Air Marshal Sir Patrick Playfair, KBE, CB, CVO before retiring; while Richard G Blomfield, an Australian-born ex-cavalry officer, who was 56 Squadron's commander when it first went to France, stayed in the RAF after the war. He eventually died on March 16th 1940 as a Wing Commander, DSO.

A few, a very few, of Albert Ball's contemporaries have survived all rigours of age and danger and, at the time of writing (1976) are still with us; men who six decades ago were vibrant young men, pioneering air combat techniques in the world's first-ever war in the newest element to be conquered by man. Men like the New Zealander, Keith L Caldwell – 'Grid' to his intimates – who was considered by many of his WWI fellow fighting pilots to have been one of the finest fighting leaders of the old RFC. In his

...as originally built at the Austin Works, May 1917

native New Zealand, Caldwell is now (1976) Air Commodore, CBE, MC, DFC, Retd.

Another who knew and flew with Ball is Squadron Leader H E Hervey, MC 'Tim' to his friends. As an Observer in 8 Squadron, RFC, Hervey had been Ball's partner in the air, and shared experiences on operations with him. After a lifetime virtually devoted to flying in every form, including the 1939-45 war period, Tim Hervey today continues to be 'air-minded'; being a stalwart member of the British Balloon and Airship Club. Yet another surviving contemporary of Ball is Wing Commander W M 'Willie' Fry, MC, whose initial meeting with Ball is recorded in the appropriate section of this narrative.

All of these men recorded their impressions of meeting and serving with Albert Ball; all have unreservedly acknowledged Ball's huge reputation as a fighting pilot, and as a modest, gentle boy whose outward manner gave little clue to the truly great fighting spirit within him. Sir Hugh Trenchard, a man little given to laudation where it was not merited, said of Ball, 'I never met a boy who was so keen on his work, more modest, or with a greater sense of his responsibility than Ball. The little I could see of him

Austin-Ball FB1, B9909, at Martlesham Heath for Service testing, mid 1917

made me realise that he was quite out of the ordinary; no task was too great for him to tackle and no little detail was too small for him to see to if it affected his work. He had a wonderfully well-balanced brain, and his loss to the Flying Corps was the greatest loss it could sustain at that time.'

One who knew Ball more intimately, his 56 Squadron commanding officer, Richard Blomfield, said of Ball, 'In the whole course of my connection with him, one fact always stands out; he never in the slightest degree presumed on his reputation. He was always keen and eager to do anything I wished, and the only trouble I ever had was in trying to keep him on the ground, when he wanted to be up in the air, fighting. To quote his own words, 'Two jobs a day are no good to me; I want to be up all the time.' However, even in this he always deferred to my ruling. He was the first airman to go right into his man and fight him to a finish crash, or be crashed – and he frequently took on heavy odds, which he overcame by his audacity in attack. He always seized the initiative and attacked, and therein in no small degree lay the secret of

Austin-Ball FB1, B9909,
after modification at Martlesham Heath with two-bay wing bracing and straightened wings

his success. He was a striking example of what courage means. His fights, in many of which his machine was so shot about that how it ever carried him back to the aerodrome was little short of a miracle, took a lot out of him, and he would go to bed exhausted as soon as possible after his return to the aerodrome.

In the Mess and in the everyday life of the squadron he was most modest and unassuming, full of fun, and undeniably popular with his fellow officers and men, all of whom swore by him and were devoted to him. He never claimed an enemy machine down 'out of control'. His were all absolute crashes that were either seen to crash by himself or by other reliable witnesses. He was as straightforward and honest as he was fearless. The moral value of his example to the squadron was incalculable; to it can safely be attributed in a large measure the success that was attained and so gallantly maintained by the squadron. He was killed, but his traditions continued to live and were the standard at which every pilot in the squadron aimed.'

Cervantes once wrote: 'History is a depository of great actions, the witness of what is past, the example and instructor of the present, and the monitor of the future'; while Beaconsfield called it, 'the legacy of heroes – the memory of a great name, and the inheritance of a great example...'

Both men could have applied these thoughts equally to Albert Ball, the Nottingham boy who inspired a nation, and left behind him a tradition of raw courage to which his successors could ever aspire.

Bronze statue of Albert Ball by Henry Poole, exhibited in the National Gallery, London

APPENDIX 1

Aircraft Flown by Albert Ball

Despite exhaustive search, the present location of Albert Ball's Flying Log Book(s) has yet to be discovered; hence the list below should not be regarded as wholly comprehensive. However, it does detail every aircraft positively known to have been flown by Ball on active service in France.

BE2c

        1707 – 8 Sqn:

        1709 – 8 Sqn:

        2498 – 8 Sqn:

        2611 – 8 Sqn: Named 'SPRINGBOK' at one period

        2625 – 13 Sqn:

        2644 – 13 Sqn:

        2657 – 8 Sqn:

        4070 – 13 Sqn:

        4076 – 13 Sqn:

        4105 – 13 Sqn:

        4136 – 8 Sqn:

        4138 – 8 Sqn:

        4173 – 13 Sqn:

        4200 – 13 Sqn:

        4352 – 13 Sqn: Arrived on unit 12/12/15

BE2d

        5735 – 8 Sqn:

        5752 – 8 Sqn:

        5799 – 8 Sqn:

        5876 – 8 Sqn:

        6252 – 8 Sqn:

BE 12

> 6495 – 8 Sqn:

Bristol Scout D

> 5313 – 13 Sqn:
> 5316 – 13 Sqn:
> 5554 – 34 (Reserve) Sqn, Orfordness:
> 5562 – 11 Sqn:
> 5563 – 11 Sqn:

Nieuport 16 and 17 Scouts

> 5173 – 11 Sqn: to 60 Sqn, 17/10/16: to 29 Sqn, 11/3/17:
> A126 – 11 Sqn: wrecked 27/5/16 and repaired at 2 AD:
> A133 – 11 Sqn: to 60 Sqn, 1/10/16: missing 26/10/16:
> A134 – 11 Sqn: to 60 Sqn, 23/8/16:
> A200 – 60 Sqn: transferred from 11 Sqn, 28/8/16: type 17:
> A201 – 11 and 60 Sqns: type 17:
> A212 – 60 Sqn: SOC 26/10/16: Type 16:
> A213 – 60 Sqn: lost 6/3/17: type 17:
> B1522 – 56 Sqn: type 17: to 1 Sqn, 7/6/17; to 29 Sqn,
> 19/8/17:

SE5

> A4850 – 56 Sqn: Ball killed 7/5/17:
> A4855 – 56 Sqn:
> A4858 – 56 Sqn:
> A8898 – 56 Sqn: delivered to unit by Ball, 1/5/17:
> to 60 Sqn, August 1917: with 40 Sqn by March 1918, and
> wrecked on 24/3/18

APPENDIX 2

The Austin AFB
('Austin-Ball Scout')

One persistent legend associated with Albert Ball is the widely-held belief that Ball designed a fighting aeroplane, the so-termed Austin-Ball Scout, to his personal ideas and for his private use in combat. As with most legends this assertion has elements of truth in basis, but past chroniclers of Ball have usually tended to confuse the true story. Their misconceptions have generally originated from misquotation of a letter which Ball wrote to his family on April 14th 1916, whilst serving with 13 Squadron RFC, in which he said:

> I have *managed to get* the plans of a most wonderful machine. It would be heaps better than the Hun Focker (*sic*). I have been to the Major and he has given me permission to fly it, if I get one out. I know that it would be a fine thing.

The full and precise wording of the original letter here (italics are the author's) indicate a rather different interpretation to that placed upon the part-quoted versions published in the past. Clearly, Ball had only stated that he had *acquired* some 'plans' for what must presumably have been a form of fighting scout, hence his comparison with the German Fokker *Eindecker* monoplane then opposing the RFC in France.

On the date he wrote his letter Ball had been in France on active flying service for exactly eight weeks. During that period he had flown only BE2c two-seat reconnaissance aircraft, on a total of 26 operational sorties over enemy-held territory; all artillery registration patrols or as 'escort' to other BEs from his unit. He had been engaged by enemy aircraft briefly on three occasions, each time without having to actually fight. He had yet to experience any fighting in any single-seat machine; indeed it was to be another two weeks (April 29th) before he made his first operational sortie in such an aircraft, when he was permitted to take the controls of 13 Squadron's only (then) Bristol Scout, D5316, for a 30-minute practice flight over his own airfield. That afternoon he took off in the Bristol for a 'patrol' over the lines, which lasted just 22 minutes and was without incident.

Ball's next flight in a single-seater was in another squadron Bristol Scout, 5313, on May 5th; and his first-ever combat in any scout machine occurred on May 15th – again, in a Bristol Scout. Thus, when Ball wrote of having '...managed to get the plans...' he had neither intimate knowledge or practical experience of any operational scout machine, and virtually no experience of aerial combat.

Ball's experience then (and later) was also totally lacking in the field of aeronautical engineering and design. Though possessing a limited knowledge of basic engineering theory and practice, he had received no training, or indeed expressed any specific interest in aeronautics from any engineering standpoint. Accordingly, though there is no question that Ball had acquired plans of some form of fighting machine by mid-April 1916, it remains a minor mystery as to precisely what form this machine took. It can be stated with certainty that it could not have been the later 'Austin-Ball Scout'.

On May 3rd 1916 Ball wrote further, 'Re-aeroplane. Plans will be sent on in a few days', but three days later he wrote again, amending his previous note by saying, 'Cannot send plans by post; so I shall bring them when I come home on leave.' In the event Ball did not get leave from France until June 10th, by which time he was serving with 11 Squadron. If indeed he took the plans home with him, no trace of these or their use (if any) has been discovered. Even had he pursued the matter of having this aeroplane actually built, assuming the plans were of a practicable project, it would be unlikely that any manufacturer would have been especially impressed with Ball's contemporary 'qualifications' as a fighting pilot of any great repute.

By September 1st 1916, when Ball next came to England on leave however, it was a different picture entirely. On that date he was serving with 60 Squadron, and had accumulated several months of first-hand fighting experience in Bristol Scouts and a Nieuport 16 Scout. His increasingly successful combat record had already established him with a high reputation, and he had been awarded a DSO and MC for his prowess. There is little doubt that his opinions and 'advice' on matters relating to fighting aeroplanes and their essential requirements were not only valued but much sought after. Indeed, a few weeks later one manufacturing concern pressed on Ball a 'retainer' of £1,000 in the hope of persuading Ball to leave the RFC and lend his prestige to their business; an offer Ball refused to entertain as long as the war was still being waged. By the time Ball finally left the fighting zone in France on posting to England (October 4th 1916), his name was known internationally, and his reputation at its peak.

His father was a director on the board of the Austin Motor Company Ltd of Birmingham, and in January 1916 had given young Albert a block of shares in the firm's stock. In that year the company was already engaged in contract work for the Government, manufacturing BE2 and RE7 aircraft, and the aeroplane building aspect was increasing in volume. Thus, when Ball made a few general sketches and an outline 'specification' of what he considered (in October 1916) to be an ideal fighter, it is hardly surprising that his father was able to impose these ideas upon the company, with a view to the firm undertaking full design and manufacture of such an aeroplane.

Ball's father handed his son's sketches and outline to the late J D North, then manager of Austin's aircraft department; and a few days later North allotted responsibility for the actual design to a member of his staff, C H Brooks. Consent for the project was given by Herbert Austin, only with the proviso that eventual official backing would be obtained from Brigadier-General Sefton Brancker at the War Office. Of the sketches North recalled, 'Young Ball's idea was basically a water-cooled Hispano-powered Nieuport (Scout) with two upward-firing guns located on a low centre-section for easy changing of magazine drums. We structured and detailed the general arrangement to more practical form.'*

The upper-wing Lewis guns installation was plainly derived from Ball's recent experience with his Nieuport Scouts in 60 Squadron in France, but North's reference to an Hispano-Suiza engine as Ball's idea is questionable. It was not until November 20th 1916 that Ball was given, officially, drawings and specifications of the 150 hp Hispano-Suiza engine; a power plant of which Ball had no previous practical knowledge.

On a slightly later date Ball did press Austin's to replace the 150 hp Hispano with a 200 hp version, and it may have been this which North was actually referring to in this context. On November 17th Lieutenant Colonel W D Beatty, Assistant Director of Aircraft Equipment in the War Office, wrote to the Austin firm,

> I am directed to inform you that it is understood you are proposing to get out the design of a fighting aeroplane on lines suggested by Captain Ball, DSO, RFC. I am to ask you to forward to us information as to the basis upon which you will be prepared to undertake this design.

The company's reply three days later was to the effect

* *British Aviation*, Vol 2 by H Penrose.

that they had, '… no knowledge of the quantities required, or details of the type.' However, on that date, November 20th, a copy of the official specification 2A was given to Ball, and a further copy despatched to Austin's on December 1st. By then preparatory design work had already begun, and Ball had visited the company to enquire about progress by December 5th, on which date he wrote to his father, 'Called at Austin's… found they had done very little about the 200 hp engine etc, so I spent three hours with War Office this morning and arranged all things.'

Two days later he was officially attached to 25 Wing HQ in order to visit Austin's officially. On December 30th the company were able to submit to the War Office full technical data, estimated performance figures, and specification as requested – an indication of efficient progress being made by the company.

After careful study of the Austin prospectus, Beatty's department put forward a generally favourable critique on January 25th 1917; and on February 7th Beatty's immediate superior was requested to contact Ball with a view to inviting him to meet Sefton Brancker and discuss the machine. It so happened that Ball was in London that day, and, without previous appointment, personally visited Brancker the following morning, before receiving the official invitation. The result of his talk with Brancker was a verbal promise for official sanction for Austin's to build two prototypes. Ball passed this information direct to the company, but was privately annoyed with the preliminary title applied to the machine by the manufacturer, as he grumbled in a letter to his father dated February 9th, 'I told Austins I was surprised at them calling the machine the Austin, and forgetting me. Also I stated it was to be called the A B, or Austin Ball.'

Written confirmation of Brancker's promise was finally sent on March 21st, and eventually Contract No 87/A/1524 issued to cover manufacture of two machines. Meanwhile, on March 15th, the Austin Company wrote to the Air Board Technical Department stating, 'These two machines are now practically completed, with the exception of main planes... and understand that the exact design of the wings is left with Captain Ball, and we have therefore written to him for particulars.' By 'design' of the wings the writer was merely referring to a decision as to whether these should be straight-edged, or with a slight sweep back from centre as (apparently) originally envisaged by Ball in his initial sketches – the latter pattern again derived from his Nieuport Scouts.

By this date Ball was a Flight commander with 56 Squadron at London Colney, working-up for an imminent move to France and thereby his return to the operational scene. Undoubtedly he was fully occupied with his new responsibilities, and therefore relegated his interest in the AFB1 to second priority in his mind. The new SE5, with which 56 was now beginning to equip, was not to Ball's liking, and on March 22nd he wrote home:

> The SE5 has turned out a dud. Its speed is only about half Nieuport speed, and it is not so fast getting up... if Austin will not buck up and finish a machine for me, I shall have to go out on SE5s and do my best.

Considering that Ball had procrastinated for nearly five months on the simple decision of the wings' pattern, his inferred accusation against Austin's of slow progress was hardly justified.

Fitted with a 200 hp Hispano-Suiza engine, the machine which finally emerged from C H Brooks' design was a neat, 'clean', one-bay little biplane with equal span, slightly swept-back wings. Its armament was drastically revised from Ball's original suggestion. Whilst the upper wing mounted a Lewis gun, as Ball had required, a second Lewis was fitted in the hollow airscrew shaft firing directly ahead. In general construction the AFB1 was conventional for its day, though particular care had been taken with detail fittings. It was allocated an official serial number, B9909, though no photos appear to exist now showing the machine thus marked. In this form the aeroplane left Austin's to proceed to Martlesham Heath for official trials on June 1st 1917 – but by then Albert Ball was dead, and the main impetus behind progress of the AFBl was gone. The test trials resulted in a variety of minor modifications, but overall the machine was favourably impressive. Its general performance compared well with the SE5, but not sufficiently to justify full-scale production apparently. In late August, for unknown reasons, its wings were replaced by straight-edged versions, braced in a similar fashion to the Spad S7 and thereby giving the false impression of a two-bay structure. In this form it was officially reported on in mid-October 1917, and finally left Martlesham Heath on October 29th bound for the depot at Ascot (minus its engine), from where, it would seem, it never emerged again. Its 'epilogue' came on November 29th 1917, on which date the machine's airframe and engine log books were despatched to the Aeronautical Inspection Directorate (AID) for retention.

It has been suggested in the past that Ball only pursued the thought of an 'ideal' aeroplane in the winter months of 1916-17 because of his frustration with the mundane and, apparently, pointless Service postings he was subjected to then. Had he been granted his wish to return to France quickly, therefore, the AFBl might never have been either conceived or built. Certainly, it was never in Ball's nature to be idle mentally or physically; his active brain and lively intellect needed constant stimulation if he was to be content with any given task or responsibility. It can only be speculation now whether, had he lived, Ball would have continued to press for the production of the machine. His growing reconciliation to the 'dud' SE5 in the final days of his service with 56 Squadron suggests otherwise.

APPENDIX 3

Award Citations

Military Cross
Extract from *London Gazette* of 27th July 1916:

For conspicuous skill and gallantry on many occasions, notably when, after failing to destroy an enemy kite balloon with bombs, he returned for a fresh supply, went back and brought it down in flames. He has done great execution among enemy aeroplanes. On one occasion he attacked six in one flight, forced down two and drove the others off. This occurred several miles over the enemy's lines.

Distinguished Service Order
Extract from *London Gazette* of 26th September 1916:

For conspicuous gallantry and skill. Observing seven enemy machines in formation, he immediately attacked machines in formation, he immediately attacked one of them and shot it down at 15 yards range. The remaining machines retired. Immediately afterwards, seeing five more hostile machines, he attacked one at about 10 yards range and shot it down, flames coming out of the fuselage. He then attacked another of the machines, which had been firing at him, and shot it down into a village, when it landed on the top of a house. He then went to the nearest aerodrome for more ammunition, and, returning, attacked three more machines, causing them to dive under control. Being then short of petrol he came home. His own machine was badly shot about in these fights.

Bar to the Distinguished Service Order
Extract from *London Gazette* of 26th September 1916:

When on escort duty to a bombing raid he saw four enemy machines in formation. He dived on to them and broke up their formation, and then shot down the nearest one, which fell on its nose. He came down to about 500 feet to make certain it was wrecked. On another occasion, observing 12 enemy machines in formation, he dived in among them, and fired a drum into the nearest machine, which went down out of control. Several more hostile machines then approached, and he fired three drums at them, driving down another out of control. He then returned, crossing the lines at a low altitude, with his machine very much damaged. (The award of the Distinguished Service Order is also announced in the *Gazette* of this date.)

Second Bar to the Distinguished Service Order
Extract from *London Gazette* of 25th November 1916:
For conspicuous gallantry in action. He attacked three hostile machines and brought one down, displaying great courage and skill. He has brought down eight hostile machines in a short period, and has forced many others to land.

Russian Order of St George, 4th Class
Extract from *London Gazette* of 16th February 1917:
Conferred by Field Marshal His Imperial Majesty the Emperor of Russia.
September 12th 1916.

ORDER OF ST GEORGE
4th Class
2nd Lt (Temp Capt) A BALL, DSO, MC, Notts and Derby Regt and RFC.
(No citation).

Honorary Freedom of the City of Nottingham
Copy Minutes of the Special Meeting of the Council, 19th February 1917:
At a Meeting of the Council of the City of Nottingham held in the Council Chamber at the Exchange Hall on

Friday, the 24th day of November, 1916, it was resolved unanimously, on the motion of the Mayor, seconded by the Sheriff:-

That Flight Commander Captain Albert Ball, DSO, MC, being a person of distinction within the meaning of the Honorary Freedom of Boroughs Act, 1885, be admitted an Honorary Freeman of the City of Nottingham, in recognition of the great services rendered by him as an Officer of the Royal Flying Corps in connection with the operations of the British Expeditionary Force in France, and as a mark of the appreciation of his fellow Citizens for his bravery in the face of the enemy.

This is to certify that Flight Commander Albert Ball has been duly admitted an Honorary Freeman of the City of Nottingham pursuant to the above resolution.

Given under the Common Seal of the said Council this 19th day of February 1917.

J E PENDLETON, Mayor
Corporation Seal
W J BOARD, Town Clerk

Legion d'Honneur, Croix de Chevalier (France)
Notified in *London Gazette* of 2nd June 1917 – No Citation.

Victoria Cross
Extract from *London Gazette* of 8th June 1917:

Lieutenant (temp Captain) Albert Ball, DSO, MC, late Notts and Derbyshire Regiment and RFC.

For most conspicuous and consistent bravery from the 25th of April to the 6th of May 1917, during which period Captain Ball took part in twenty-six combats in the air and destroyed eleven hostile aeroplanes, drove down two out of control, and forced several others to land. In these combats Captain Ball, flying alone, on one occasion fought six hostile machines, twice he fought five, and once four. When leading two other British aeroplanes he attacked an enemy formation of eight. On each of these occasions he brought down at least one enemy. Several times his aeroplane was badly damaged, once so seriously that but for the most delicate handling his machine would have collapsed, as nearly all the control wires had been shot away. On returning with a damaged machine he had always to be restrained from immediately going out on another.

In all, Captain Ball has destroyed forty-three German aeroplanes and one balloon, and has always displayed most exceptional courage, determination and skill.

APPENDIX 4

Combat Record of Albert Ball

The following tabulation of combats in which Ball is known to have participated relates only to those in which he did, could, or might have reasonably claimed a 'victory', moral or physical. Devotees of the 'ace' cult, so prevalent among aviation enthusiasts since World War 1, will undoubtedly make their own individual interpretations here, with the, to me, pointless objective of establishing a 'score'. The entire question of any fighter pilot's tally ('score') of victories in aerial combat is, to say the least, highly contentious. Any combination from a hundred unrelated variables could affect whether one pilot achieves a relatively high number of so-termed 'victories'; yet an equally skilled, aggressive pilot, by comparison, achieves few or none.

It should be quite apparent to an objective reader that the quality of any fighter pilot's greatness, prowess, and/or leadership instinct is impossible to judge simply by the criterion of a claimed 'score'. Equally, the comparatively few fighter pilots of the 1914–18 aerial war who did accumulate a number of officially accredited victories were not simply lucky. Experience, skill, instinctive aggressiveness, guile – all played a part in achieving the status of 'ace', a term, incidentally, loudly derided by members of the British flying services.

It should be noted too that the majority of claimed, and thereafter officially credited, 'victories' by pilots of World War I came in the category 'Out of Control'; the official term for an enemy machine seen to fall, apparently thoroughly defeated, but whose end is not actually witnessed. This fact should be borne well in mind by those who merely interpret a 'victory' as meaning the complete destruction of an aircraft.

The following list of Ball's combats gives only the salient reference details of date, aircraft flown by Ball, German aircraft involved (where known), and result as far as this can be intelligently ascertained from available evidence. The majority of these combats are detailed more deeply within the text. All times quoted are in terms of the Service 24-hour clock system, and relate to British time. Where two times are coupled thus, 0715–0830 hrs, these are the parameters of the specific patrol or sortie.

Abbreviations used:

C-type	–Two-seater aircraft
D-type	–Single-seat biplane
E-type	–*Eindecker*, or monoplane
KB	–Kite Observation Balloon
DD	–Driven down
FTL	–Forced to land
OOC	–Out of control
WIA	–Wounded in action
KIA	–Killed in action
POW	–Prisoner of war

Note: Specific identification of German aircraft by Ball was not always accurate; understandably so in the heat of a combat, and in the light of the very small amount of official training or reference then in enemy aircraft recognition. On September 21st and 22nd 1916, Ball reported 'Roland single-seaters' as his opponents; when in fact he was fighting a Fokker DIII on the latter date. The first Roland D-types did not reach front-line units until after these dates. Again, on October 1st, 1916 he reported his opponent as a 'Roland single-seater'; when he was probably fighting either a Fokker DIII or even an Albatros DI or DII.

Another new type of German single-seater scout was also beginning to appear on the Western Front in the autumn of 1916 – the Halberstadt DII – the shape of which differed significantly from the various aircraft Ball had encountered. Again, although Ball may well have been correct in identifying a large proportion of his two-seater opponents as Albatros Cs, they might just as easily have been other makes then being used on operations over France, with a generally similar configuration; such as the Rumpler CI and early DFW C-types. The one type on which Ball was positive was the Roland CII two-seater, with its uniquely-located two-man crew, and interplane I-strutting.

Combat Record of Albert Ball

Squadron	Aircraft	Date 1916	Hostile	Remarks
13	BE2c, 4200	April 10	KB	Driven down. 0925–1147 hrs.
13	BE2c, 4070	April 29	Albatros C	Shot down by Ball's observer, Lt S A Villiers. FTL, with German observer WIA or KIA 0515–0755 hrs.
11	Bristol Scout 5313	May 15	Albatros C	OOC. Claimed by Ball in letter home.
11	Bristol Scout	May 16	Albatros C	FTL. German observer WIA.
11	Nieuport A126	May 22	Albatros C	Driven down.
11	Nieuport A126	May 22	LVG C	FTL.
11	Nieuport 5173	May 29	LVG C	Driven down. 0800 hrs. Last seen falling vertically.
11	Nieuport 5173	May 29	LVG C	FTL. 0830 hrs.
11	Nieuport 5173	June 1	LVG C	FTL. 1010 hrs.
11	Nieuport 5173	June 1	Fokker E	FTL. 1015 hrs.
11	Nieuport 5173	June 25	KB	In flames. 1600 hrs. Used phosphor bombs.
11	Nieuport A134	July 2	Roland CII	Crashed. 1730 hrs.
11	Nieuport A134	July 2	Aviatik C	Crashed. 1800 hrs.
11	Nieuport A134	July 3	KB	FTL. Attacked with Le Prieur rockets and gun. Apparently undamaged.
8	BE2c 5876	August 9	KB	Forced German observer to jump by parachute. 1130–1220 hrs.
8	BE2c 5876	August 12	Albatros C	Driven down. No visible result. 1330–1543 hrs. No observer carried by Ball.
11	Nieuport A201	August 16	Roland CII	OOC. 0910 hrs.

11	Nieuport A201	August 16	Roland CII	Driven down. 0920 hrs.
11	Nieuport A201	August 16	Roland CII	Driven down. 0930 hrs.
11	Nieuport A201	August 22	Roland CII	Crashed. 1900–1930 hrs.
11	Nieuport A201	August 22	Roland CII	Crashed. German observer POW. 1900–1930 hrs.
60	Nieuport A201	August 25	Roland CII	OOC.
60	Nieuport A201	August 25	Roland CII	OOC.
60	Nieuport A201	August 25	Roland CII	Crashed.
60	Nieuport A201	August 28	Roland CII	FTL. German pilot KIA. 0915–0945 hrs.
60	Nieuport A201	August 28	Roland CII or LVG C	FTL. 1830–1930 hrs. 'Seemed quite uncrashed' (*sic*).
60	Nieuport A201	August 28	Roland CII	FTL. 1830–1930 hrs.
60	Nieuport A201	August 28	Roland CII	Crashed. 1830–1930 hrs.
60	Nieuport A201	August 28	C-type	Driven down. 1830–1930 hrs.
60	Nieuport A201	August 31	Roland CII	Crashed 1830 hrs.
60	Nieuport A201	August 31	Roland CII	FTL. 2020 hrs.
60	Nieuport A200	September 15	D-type	Crashed. 0955 hrs.
60	Nieuport A212	September 15	Albatros C	FTL. 1500 hrs. German observer WIA.
60	Nieuport A201	September 15	Roland CII	Crashed. 1900 hrs. Both Germans WIA.
60	Nieuport A213	September 19	Albatros C	FTL. 1815 hrs.
60	Nieuport A213	September 21	D-type	FTL. 1530–1630 hrs.
60	Nieuport A213	September 21	D-type	Crashed. 1530–1630 hrs.
60	Nieuport A213	September 21	Roland CII	Crashed. 1715–1830 hrs.
60	Nieuport A213	September 22	Roland CII	FTL. 1130 hrs.

Sqn	Aircraft	Date	Enemy	Notes
60	Nieuport A213	September 22	Fokker DIII	Crashed. 1640–1805 hrs. German pilot KIA. Ball did not see finish, but 'thought most likely destroyed'.
60	Nieuport A213	September 22	Roland CII	Driven down. 1640–1805 hrs. No result seen.
60	Nieuport A213	September 23	Albatros C	Crashed burning. Just after 1800 hrs.
60	Nieuport A213	September 25	Albatros C	Crashed. Pilot WIA, Observer KIA. Ball ran out of ammunition and did not claim. 1800–1845 hrs.
60	Nieuport A213	September 26	Roland CII or Albatros C	Driven down, 'under control' (sic). Observer thought WIA or KIA. 1800 hrs.
60	Nieuport A213	September 28	Albatros C	Crashed. 1745 hrs.
60	Nieuport A213	September 28	Roland CII or Albatros C	FTL. 1810–1915 hrs.
60	Nieuport A213	September 28	Roland CII or Albatros C	FTL. 1810–1915 hrs.
60	Nieuport A201	September 30	Albatros C	Fell in flames. 1055 hrs. Officially credited as shared with 11 Sqn FE2b crew.
60	Nieuport A213	September 30	Roland CII	OOC. 1800–1845 hrs. 'Thought it must have crashed' (sic).
60	Nieuport A213	October 1	Albatros D	FTL. 0710–0730 hrs.
60	Nieuport A213	October 1	Albatros C	FTL. 0735–0825 hrs.
60	Nieuport	October 1	Albatros C	FTL. 0735–0825 hrs.
		1917		
56	Nieuport B1522	April 23	Albatros C	Crashed, 0600–0835 hrs.
56	SE5 A4850	April 23	Albatros DIII	In flames. 1045–1400 hrs.
56	SE5 A4850	April 23	Albatros C	FTL. 1045–1400 hrs. Observer WIA and died later date.
56	SE5 A4850	April 26	Albatros DIII	Crashed. 1815–2035 hrs.
56	SE5 A4850	April 26	Albatros DIII	Crashed in flames. 1815–2035 hrs.

56	SE5 A4850	April 28	Albatros C	FTL. 1600–1825 hrs. 'Apparently OK' (*sic*).
56	SE5 A4850	April 28	Albatros C	Crashed. 1600–1815 hrs.
56	SE5 A8898	May 1	Albatros C	Crashed. 1810–2030 hrs.
56	SE5 A8898	May 1	Albatros C	FTL. 1810–2030 hrs.
56	SE5 A4855	May 2	Albatros DIII	Crashed. 1830–2030 hrs.
56	SE5 A4855	May 2	Albatros C	OOC. Observer POW. Ball did not see finish. 2010 hrs.
56	SE5 A8898	May 4	Albatros DIII	Crashed. 1750–2030 hrs.
56	SE5 A8898	May 5	Albatros DIII	Crashed. 1800–1910 hrs.
56	SE5 A8898	May 5	Albatros DIII	Crashed. 1800–1910 hrs.
56	Nieuport B1522	May 6	Albatros DIII	Crashed. Pilot seriously injured. 1900–2040 hrs.

APPENDIX 5

Memorabilia

Memorabilia of Albert Ball exists today (1976) in a surprisingly large variety of locations. Fortunately for the historian and general 'enthusiast', many such items can be viewed without fuss or trouble in certain public institutions, while others, understandably, are purely private and personal mementoes preserved very carefully by individuals who were related to, or knew Ball intimately. In respect of such privacy, the list which follows relates solely to those items freely available for inspection by members of the public in easily-accessible institutions, providing certain simple conditions are fulfilled, such as an appointment or, simply, a normal entrance fee is paid, whichever may be applicable. Each item listed is authenticated and a genuine Ball 'memento'.

Nottingham Castle Museum
    Complete medals and awards, including Victoria Cross.
    Medal of Aero Club of America, awarded post-1918.
    Freedom of Nottingham Scroll and Casket.
    Posthumous Scroll and Medal.
    Wrist identity bracelet in 9-carat gold.
    Royal Aero Club Certificate.
    Wristwatch, NCM 1966–70, 18-carat gold.
    Webley revolver.
    Colt automatic pistol.
    Silver cigarette case, initialled 'A B'.
    Black fountain pen.
    Wing pennant from one of Ball's aircraft.
    Message tube, with streamers, dropped by Germans to notify death.
    Avro windshield, pierced by bullet-hole.
    Engine induction pipe (section), showing bullet

damage – from Nieuport Scout, 5173 after combat on
June 25th, 1916.
Original sketch of one of Ball's Nieuport Scouts, with
spinner, 60 Squadron, by Roderic Hill.
Original oil painting.
Miscellaneous letters and photographs.
Original combat reports, framed.

Imperial War Museum, London
Service dress uniform and breeches, with Captain's
rank insignia.
Leather flying helmet.
Pair of thin leather gloves.
Service hat.
Portion of damaged SE5 radiator.
Two fuselage spars, broken (approximately 12-inches
long) from SE5, A4850.
Section of propeller, with signature.
Small compass.
Lieutenant's rank insignia.
Medal ribbons.
Small, crumpled cigarette case.

Royal Air Force Museum, Hendon, near London.
RFC 'wings' brevet, cut from tunic.
Penknife and fountain pen – from Ball's body.
Two pencils – from Ball's body.
One Pound Sterling Treasury note – from Ball's body.
Lewis .303 machine gun, No 9134E (reputed to be from
one of Ball's SE5s, but this is extremely doubtful).

Trent College, Long Eaton, Nottinghamshire
Original cross (German-made) from Ball's grave – in
College Chapel.
Propeller from one of Ball's 60 Squadron Nieuport
Scouts – probably Nieuport 5173 – mounted in Dining
Hall.
Original Denholm Davies oil portrait – in the May Hall.

56 Squadron, Royal Air Force

Full RFC dress uniform, with cap and gloves – in case.
Clock, mounted in hub of propeller from SE5, A4850, and presented to unit by Sir Albert Ball.
Log Books (engine and airframe) for SE5, A4850 – presented to unit by Wing Commander T B Marson.
Miscellaneous photos, letters, documents.

11 Squadron, Royal Air Force

Original combat reports.

The following items, all extracted from the wreckage of SE5, A4850 on May 7th, 1917, were initially given to Lothar von Richthofen, and were transferred to the Richthofen home at Schweidnitz, Germany. After Lothar's death in 1922, all were mounted and displayed in a room specifically dedicated to Lothar's memory; and remained so until 1944 when invading Russian Army units caused the Baronin von Richthofen to flee to the west, leaving virtually everything. It was next reported that all items of historic nature were transferred from Schweidnitz to the Moscow Air Museum, but no confirmation has been made of the present location (if any) of the items.

Vickers .303 machine gun, No A541.
Two Very Light pistols.
Ammunition belt section (from Vickers machine gun).
Section of petrol pipe, cut by bullet scar.
Various instruments from SE5's dashboard.
All other mementoes are retained privately by individuals.

Bibliography

All historical research leans heavily upon reference to books, documents, records. The following were principally consulted in the course of my research; though it should not be taken for granted that I believed all I read without query. Blind faith in the printed word too often fortifies fanciful legend; whereas the aim of the historian, if he is worthy of the description, is unequivocal seeking for truth.

Captain Ball, VC, W.A.Briscoe & H.R.Stannard; H Jenkins, 1918
The Boy Hero, W.A.Briscoe; Milford, 1920
Albert Ball, VC, DSO, R.H.Kiernan; John Hamilton, 1933
War in the Air, Vol 2 H.A.Jones; Oxford University Press, 1928
History of 60 Squadron, A.J.L.Scott; Heinemann, 1919
Sixty Squadron, 1916-66, D.W.Warne & A.J.Young; 1967
Scarlet and Khaki, T.B.Marson; Jonathan Cape, 1930
Trent College, 1868-1927, M.A.J.Tarver; G.Bell & Sons, 1929
Wind in the Wires, D.Grinnel-Milne; Hurst & Blackett, 1933
Sagittarius Rising, C.Lewis; Peter Davies, 1936
The Red Air Fighter, Manfred von Richthofen; Aeroplane, 1918
Flying and Soldiering, R.R.Money; Nicholson & Watson, 1936
Flying Fever, S.F.Vincent; Jarrolds, 1972
Air of Battle, W.M.Fry; William Kimber Ltd, 1974
Observer, A.J.Insall, William Kimber Ltd, 1970
RFC HQ, (Revised edition), M.Baring; Blackwood, 1968

Pioneer Pilot, F.D.Tredrey; Peter Davies, 1976
Fighters of WW1, Vol 1, (Revised), J.M.Bruce;
Macdonald, 1965
British Aviation, Vol 2, H.Penrose; Putnam, 1969
History of 56 Squadron, 1916-19, G.C.Maxwell;
Unpublished MS
11 Squadron Diary, 1916, W.E.G.Crisford;
Unpublished MS
Knight of Germany, Professor J.Werner, John
Hamilton Ltd, 1933

Periodicals:
Popular Flying, Ed W.E.Johns, 1932-38, Various
Journal of Cross and Cockade Society, Various,
1959-76
Flying, Ed W.E.Johns, 1938-39, Various
Nottinghamshire Guardian, Various, 1914-17
Royal Air Force Quarterly, Various, 1930-39

Index